BEST RESUMES
FOR ATTORNEYS

BEST RESUMES
FOR ATTORNEYS

Joan Fondell
Mary Jo Russo

Russo and Fondell,
Legal Search Consultants,
Beverly Hills, California and
Santa Fe, New Mexico

John Wiley & Sons, Inc.

New York ▪ Chichester ▪ Brisbane ▪ Toronto ▪ Singapore

Library of Congress Cataloging-in-Publication Data:

Fondell, Joan, 1959–
    Best resumes for attorneys / by Joan Fondell and Mary Jo Russo.
      p.   cm.
    Includes index.
    ISBN 0-471-30922-2 (cloth : alk. paper). — ISBN 0-471-30920-6
    (paper : alk. paper)
      1. Law—Vocational guidance—United States.
    2. Resumés (Employment) I. Russo, Mary Jo, 1946–   . II. Title.
    KF297.F66   1994
    340'.023'73—dc20   93-11062

Printed in the United States of America

10 9 8 7 6 5 4 3 2 1

Disclaimer

All the resume examples in this book are fictitious. Any references to law schools, undergraduate colleges or universities, law firms or corporations, or personal data are purely fictional and were created to illustrate examples. Any resemblance to actual persons, places, or circumstances is purely coincidental.

Acknowledgments

We would like to express our gratitude to Anne Kerwin of Kerwin Associates, San Francisco, California, and Konrad L. Trope, Esq., of Trope, Trope and Associates, Beverly Hills, California, for their assistance with our research. We also thank our friends and families, who have encouraged us throughout this project.

We appreciate the effort of our Editor, Mike Hamilton for recognizing the value of this project. We also thank Nancy Marcus Land of Publications Development Company for her meticulous editing. We want to thank B.S.F. for her delicious meals, which kept us nourished throughout the writing of this book. We are extremely grateful to Sarah Schwartz for her tireless effort on the computer and for her editing assistance.

Contents

Introduction

Although attorneys are among the highest academic achievers, many are still unaware of the strategies involved in preparing an interview-getting resume. Attorneys can greatly increase their chances of finding new employment if they understand and utilize the elements of a concise, yet informative, resume.

As legal search consultants for a combined total of 23 years, we have assisted thousands of attorneys locate new jobs. Being in the legal marketplace on a daily basis, we are exceedingly aware that attorneys are generally unfamiliar and uncomfortable with the process of preparing a resume. Up to now, no book has been available that accurately reflects and specifically instructs attorneys in preparing a resume so as to highlight the information legal employers want to see. This book is designed to fill that need as well as to provide assistance with the other elements of the job search.

We have witnessed significant changes in the legal profession and its hiring practices. Unlike legal employers during most of the 1980s, law firms and corporations are no longer actively pursuing job applicants. Instead, they look for top credentialed attorneys with special niche practice area expertise. Law firms seek out partners with large books of business, controlling a large and established client base. Many feel that the practice of law has significantly changed from a scholarly profession to a bottom-line-oriented business. This debate will likely continue.

You need to be aware that you will be competing with hundreds of applicants for any attorney job opening you pursue, whether you are responding to an ad, following up on a friend's tip, or using a legal search consultant. We say this, not to frighten you, but to impress on you the importance of a clean, uncluttered, and concise resume that accurately and strategically emphasizes your strengths and attributes.

1

The Attorney Resume—What Makes It Different?

The unique quality of the Attorney resume reflects the genesis of a legal career. Students usually begin contemplating law school study during high school, and the competitiveness of law school admissions magnifies considerations of where to attend college. Then, while attending a well-respected college or university, a prelaw student must constantly keep in mind that getting good grades is essential to law school admission. Stellar performance in college must be coupled with strong L.S.A.T. scores.

Academic demands in college and the L.S.A.T. pale in comparison with the cerebral demands placed on the first-year law student. The pressure to succeed in the first year is apparent in law school classrooms, where every student joins other gifted minds all competing for the same top grades. The pressure of law school, however, is no greater than the pressure experienced by those trying to get on Law Review, either by their strong first-year grades or by the "write-on" competition. The next goal is to finish all three years of law school with a strong final class standing. While high academic standing is important, it still means little without passing the state bar. Obviously, without this final achievement, the practice of law is elusive. And, throughout the student's academic life, all his or her achievements have been or will be scrutinized by present or future employers.

Unlike other professions, the legal profession largely consists of employers who are attorneys like yourself. They have traveled an academic road that resembles your own. Hence, the attorney who considers hiring you will judge you as his or her peer.

The recession forced legal employers to evaluate the efficiency of their professional staff. In the 1980s, "big was better," and law firm mergers were abundant, creating megafirms. In the past few years, however, law firms have been rethinking that adage. Today, most law firms believe "small is more efficient." By being "lean and mean," they can function more economically and provide cost-effective legal services to their clients. As a result, law firms have downsized through layoffs and reduced hiring, both at the law school level and laterally.

While many still believe there are too many attorneys, Law School Admission Services reports that 92,500 applicants sought entry in the fall of 1992 to the 175 accredited law schools, and in 1991 over 38,000 received law degrees from accredited schools (see Philip Hager, "Attorney Glut Forces Many to Scale Back Expectation: Would-Be Lawyers Face a Job Market That Offers Less Money, Less Glitz and Few Openings in Big Cities," *Los Angeles Times*, A1, November 28, 1992). Generally, legal employers are having difficulty absorbing the current law school graduates. With large numbers of practitioners continuing to flood the market, legal employment opportunities diminish in number. Hence, creating an interview-getting resume is critical to your success.

APPEARANCE—THE PROFESSIONAL WAY TO FORMAT YOUR RESUME

Because your resume is the first opportunity to impress a potential employer, you should use a clear and concise format for your resume. Such a design will highlight your educational and professional accomplishments. Cluttering up your resume with everything you've ever done diffuses its impact.

Although the format we suggest is not the *only* way you can set up your resume, it is the format our attorney candidates have used successfully to locate legal positions. Many of the sample resumes in this book are patterned after resumes of attorneys we have worked with; however, the information has been altered to protect confidentiality.

Your resume should appear on 8½" × 11" white bond paper. A 20- to 24-pound stock is preferable. Your resume should have equal left and right margins; usually one inch is ideal. Your top and bottom margins also should be balanced; again, one inch will provide sufficient white space. Set off each section of your resume with one to two lines of extra space. This consistent spacing will make it easier for the reader to discern the information.

With the advent of personal computers (PCs), most attorneys today draft their own resume, unless they seek assistance from a legal search consultant. If you have access to a PC, it is not necessary to have your resume typeset. However, have your resume printed on a laser printer rather than on a dot matrix printer. Photocopies of a laser-printed resume are professional looking, if you choose a good-quality bond paper.

Choosing a typeface (font) can be confusing because many fonts are now available. We recommend that you pick a conservative font such as Geneva, Palatino, Times, or Bookman. The size of the print should be 10 point. The reproduced resumes in Chapter 8 were reduced to fit the book page. Full-sized, they would be 25 percent larger.

While the appearance of your resume says a great deal about you, a resume free of misspelled words, typographical errors, and grammatical errors says much more.

LENGTH—WHY BREVITY IS PREFERABLE

A shorter resume is always preferable to a longer one, if for no other reason than it takes less time to read. In the competitive job market today, recruiting coordinators, attorneys at law firms, and corporate human resource departments have neither the time nor the inclination to sift through hundreds of two- and three-page resumes. The time spent looking at a resume is a flash, often not exceeding 30 seconds. The resume either sparks interest immediately or not at all. Usually, trained recruitment staff already know what they are looking for in terms of educational and professional experience. Therefore, as we will continue to stress throughout this book, prominently setting up the educational, professional experience, and employment history sections of your resume is most critical.

A clear and concise one-page resume usually should be sufficient. If you are a partner-level attorney or a senior-level attorney, the use of a second page may not be a detriment. However, if you are a recent graduate or junior attorney and are balking at the thought of putting all your accomplishments on one page, then we recommend that you test the necessity of the information you have on the second or third page by asking yourself the following questions:

1. Have you briefly identified the most significant and valuable educational achievements?

2. Have you succinctly described your professional experience, with particular emphasis on the area of practice that you are presently applying for?

3. Have you briefly listed the significant and applicable employers you have worked for in the legal profession and given only the name, city, state, and positions held?

4. Have you briefly stated your bar admission information?

5. Have you included the "References Available Upon Request" sentence?

If you have followed all the preceding guidelines and still need to use a second page, then ask yourself whether you are putting in excludable information. If you have not included the "excludable," then use the second page to complete your resume (items such as published articles or books can be included either in your resume or as an addendum).

Again, there is no steadfast rule about one-page or two-page resumes. However, since time is money and lawyers are busy people, brevity and clarity are welcome commodities.

DESCRIBING YOUR LEGAL EXPERIENCE WITH ACTION WORDS

In writing your resume, use terms from the following list of strong, definitive words to describe your professional legal experience. Examine the list and select the words that best reflect your experience; then use them to complete your Professional Experience paragraph.

acquire	argue	conduct
act	assimilate	consolidate
administer	assist	construct
admit	augment	consult
advise	authorize	contract
advocate	chair	contribute
allocate	coach	control
analyze	collect	coordinate
appear	communicate	correct
approve	complete	counsel
arbitrate	conceptualize	create

defend	instruct	query
delegate	interface	question
demonstrate	interpret	recommend
depose	interview	recruit
determine	lead	report
develop	lease	represent
direct	lecture	request
dispose	litigate	require
distribute	locate	research
document	lose	resolve
draft	maintain	responsible for
edit	manage	review
effect	market	revise
enact	mediate	schedule
establish	modify	screen
examine	monitor	secure
execute	negotiate	set up
exercise	notify	solve
evaluate	officiate	structure
file	organize	summarize
follow-up	oversee	supervise
form	participate	supply
formulate	perform	support
forward	persuade	syndicate
furnish	plan	take
generate	prepare	train
guide	present	transact
identify	procure	transfer
implement	produce	translate
include	promote	utilize
inform	propose	verify
initiate	protect	win
institute	provide	

2

Resume Organization

In an Attorney resume, the information should be presented in a concise, straightforward style to get the employer's attention. The chronological format usually works best. Arranging information in inverse chronological order, this resume begins with the most recent experience and moves back through each preceding experience.

WHAT TO INCLUDE

Every resume should include the following information:

- ▶ Name, Address, and Home Phone Number.
- ▶ Professional Experience paragraph.
- ▶ Education, Degrees, and Honors paragraph.
- ▶ Employment History paragraph.
- ▶ Bar Admission(s) paragraph.
- ▶ "References Available Upon Request" sentence.

Name, Address, and Home Phone Number

Your name, address, and home phone number should appear, centered, at the top of your resume, approximately one inch from the top margin, and should be in boldface. One line for each entry is sufficient. Your name should be in capital letters. Your street address, city, and state should be typed with capital and lower-case letters, spelling the state out. Your area code and phone number should appear next. If you do not want to have your confidentiality breached with your present employer, do not include your work phone number.

For example, the information at the top of your resume should appear like this:

JOHN ALLAN SMITH
321 Main Street
San Francisco, California 92222
(415) 555-4341

Professional Experience Paragraph

The Professional Experience paragraph highlights your legal experience. This paragraph is particularly useful to a potential employer for it documents your experience in your area of expertise and streamlines your resume. If you have practiced within the same area of expertise for more than one year and with more than one employer, you should prepare a Professional Experience paragraph, rather than repeat your experience under each past employment opportunity. The area of practice should appear in capital letters, underlined, and may be bold or italic.

For example, a real estate development attorney would briefly describe the kinds of transactions he or she has participated in rather than to describe them each individually within the Employment History paragraph. If you opt to provide a detailed Professional Experience paragraph, then your Employment History paragraph will only need to include the dates of employment, the names and cities of your employers, and the title you held in those positions.

Such a Professional Experience paragraph might look like this:

PROFESSIONAL EXPERIENCE

REAL ESTATE DEVELOPMENT PRACTICE. General representation of real estate developers and investors in commercial, mixed use, and residential developments; including office buildings, industrial and warehousing facilities, shopping centers, hotels, and residential subdivisions. This representation includes negotiation and documentation of all matters related to acquisition and disposition of properties, space and ground leases, construction and permanent financings, and formation of partnerships and joint ventures, and also involves subdivision map work, governmental entitlement, and regulatory work.

Education, Degrees, and Honors Paragraph

As previously stated, your education should appear in reverse chronological order, beginning with your law degree. If you received a related legal degree, such as an LL.M. after your law school graduation, then list it before your J.D. degree. If you received a joint degree, such as a J.D./M.B.A., list them together. Any honors or authored publication acknowledgment should be included below the appropriate degree. If you have many publication acknowledgments, you may prefer to list them under a separate heading, "Publications."

Each degree should include the date of graduation, the degree received, the major field of study, approximate class rank or grade point average, or honorary designation. Only scholastic activities should be included.

You may choose to type the names of the universities that you attended in bold, leaving the rest of the entries below, in regular typeface.

An Education paragraph should appear like this:

EDUCATION: **University of California, Los Angeles School of Law**
Los Angeles, California
J.D. 1989
Order of the Coif
Editor, *U.C.L.A. Law Review*

University of California, at Berkeley
Berkeley, California
B.A. *magna cum laude*, Political Science, 1986

To indicate an advanced legal degree, use this format:

EDUCATION: **New York University School of Law**
New York, New York
LL.M. Taxation, 1986

Cornell University School of Law
Ithaca, New York
J.D. 1985
Class Rank: Approximately Top 25%

University of Pennsylvania
Philadelphia, Pennsylvania
B.A. *magna cum laude*, English, 1982

Employment History Paragraph

The Employment History paragraph should appear in reverse chronological order, beginning with your present employment. If, however, you provide a detailed Professional Experience paragraph, then your Employment History paragraph will be less detailed. The dates of employment should appear in the far left margin. Across from the dates of employment, you should list the complete name and city of your employer. On the next line, you should state the position you held. Repeat this same process for each legal employment position. If there are time gaps between employment, you will need to address this issue in a cover letter or during a screening interview.

For example, if you opt to prepare a Professional Experience paragraph, your Employment History paragraph might appear like this:

EMPLOYMENT:

January 1990   **Smith & Jones**
to Present   Los Angeles, California
                  Associate.

October 1988   **Green, Brown & White**
to December 1989 Los Angeles, California
                  Associate.

If you decide not to provide a Professional Experience paragraph, then you should briefly state what practice area you have worked in and describe your legal experience under each employment listing. Your present employment paragraph should be written in the present tense. Your previous employment should be written in the past tense.

For example, your Employment History paragraph might appear like this:

EMPLOYMENT:

January 1990 to Present	**Smith & Jones** Los Angeles, California
	Real Estate Finance Associate. Represent institutional lenders, developers, and other clients. Document and negotiate a variety of transactions including construction and permanent loan financing; loan financing involving multistate real property security and loan workouts; formation of partnerships and real property acquisition; ground leasing, office leasing, and retail leasing.
October 1988 to December 1989	**Green, Brown & White** Los Angeles, California Litigation Associate. Primary responsibilities included all aspects of discovery. Reviewed and drafted various motions and pleadings, and argued motions in state and federal court. Have taken and defended depositions and have prepared a case for trial.

Bar Admission(s) Paragraph

While many resume preparers overlook the Bar Admission paragraph, it is an important part of your resume. It informs a potential employer of the state(s) you are licensed to practice in, as well as the dates of admission.

If you are a litigator, you may list the courts that you are admitted to.

For example, your Bar Admission paragraph might appear like this:

BAR ADMISSIONS(S): State Bar of California, 1989. Admitted in the United States District Court for the Central, Northern, Southern and Eastern Districts of California; U.S. Court of Appeals for the Ninth Circuit.

Another example could appear like this:

BAR ADMISSION(S):   State Bars of New York, 1988; Pennsylvania 1990.

"References Available Upon Request" Sentence

Every resume you send to a prospective employer should state that you will provide references upon request. That does not mean you should list the names of your references on your resume. It does mean that you have references and will present them to an interested employer at the appropriate time.

The reference availability sentence should appear centered, in bold capital letters, and at the bottom of your resume, just above the bottom margin of the page:

REFERENCES AVAILABLE UPON REQUEST

WHAT SHOULD APPEAR FIRST—EDUCATION OR EMPLOYMENT HISTORY PARAGRAPH?

Now that we know the essential items in a resume, let's strategize the placement of your Education or Employment History paragraph to emphasize your strongest asset. The Education and Employment History paragraphs are perhaps the two most important sections in your resume. These are the paragraphs that potential employers focus on. In the flash of a moment spent evaluating and screening your resume, the prospective employer will study the education and employment history paragraphs to determine whether you are qualified for the job. Therefore, the placement of these paragraphs is critical.

As the job applicant, only you know whether your educational background or your employment history is your strongest asset. Unless you are fortunate enough to have equally strong and well-credentialed education and employment history areas, you need to determine objectively which paragraph is stronger and more impressive. Place that first, near the top of your resume, following your professional experience paragraph.

While this process is subjective, there are some objective guidelines. As you may already be aware, the Gourman Report, annually revised, is a rating of graduate and professional programs in American and International Universities. While some professional legal organizations do not endorse the Gourman Report as a means of classifying law schools, many law firms and corporations continue to use it as a reference source. Employers that do not directly consult the Gourman Report, nevertheless have a sense of which law schools are the most highly rated. In any event, you need to take this issue into consideration when creating your resume.

Equally subjective is the matter of your legal employment experience. While you may believe that the experience you received at your present or past employers is impressive, you must objectively compare your experience with other comparable legal employers. Even among law firms and corporations, there is a hierarchical sense of which law firms and corporations hire "the cream of the crop."

Taking these factors into consideration will help you determine whether your law school or your legal employment history is the most impressive.

A common situation is that of someone who attended a top law school but finished with a class rank of Top Third or below. The issue is often further complicated because the attorney is working for a well-respected big city law firm. Usually, this circumstance is the result of a law student who finished his or her first year of law school with a Top 10% class standing but had a much lower standing at graduation. The firm, already having offered this associate a job, does not renege on it; however, when the associate is pursuing other employment, he or she is in a difficult position. The question arises: Is graduation from a top law school with a lower class standing stronger or weaker than experience at the accomplished law firm? In this case, our usual recommendation would be to include the employment history paragraph first, it being stronger. Generally speaking, the theory is that well-respected law firms have good reputations for training young associates. Today, training associates is such an expensive proposition that prospective employers are relieved and excited to hire an already well-trained young legal mind.

We strongly believe that you know, inherently, which aspect of your resume is the strongest. Use it strategically and wisely to open the door to a new job opportunity.

NONESSENTIAL ITEMS THAT YOU MAY WANT TO INCLUDE

In addition to the essential items on your resume, the following list of items requires more discretion on your part. You should evaluate the potential list of what you *may* include to determine whether these additional paragraphs will enhance your resume and make you more marketable for the particular position you have in mind. Merely including such facts because they do not hurt your resume is not an adequate reason. Consider this matter carefully, because cluttering up your resume only distracts the reader from focusing on the strongest items. Let's discuss each of the discretionary paragraphs, evaluating when inclusion will strengthen your resume.

Your resume *may* include the following items:

▸ Language Capability paragraph.

▸ Personal Interests paragraph.

▸ Professional Affiliations/Associations paragraph.

▸ Publication(s) paragraph.

Language Capability Paragraph

The Language Capability paragraph is a brief listing of the languages that you have fluency in, either in written or spoken word. It should not include languages that you know only casually. Keep in mind that fluency in French, Spanish, or German does not necessarily enhance or make your resume more marketable, unless you are applying to a law firm or corporation seeking attorneys with these language skills.

For example, if you are applying to a law firm or corporation with a large client base in Latin America, Eastern Europe, or French Canada, there may be significant reason to include the preceding languages in your resume, cover letter, or both. However, if the position you are applying for has, instead, primarily a Japanese client base, fluency in German may be irrelevant. In any job position you apply for, always ask yourself whether each item in your resume enhances your marketability. If not, then you should carefully consider whether its inclusion hinders your goal of keeping your resume to one powerful page.

A language paragraph should look like this:

LANGUAGE(S):   Fluency in Mandarin and Cantonese.

Personal Interests Paragraph

The Personal Interests paragraph allows you to include the personal hobbies, sports, and activities that you enjoy. Many attorneys include a brief personal interest statement, in the hope that the interviewer will share some personal interests with the interviewee, thus making the interview go more smoothly.

Hobbies such as stamp or coin collecting, photography, and cooking are appropriate as are sports such as skiing, tennis, and basketball. Ballroom dancing, jogging, hiking, and traveling are also popular activities. Any of these may entice and interest your interviewer into engaging in a casual conversation of personal interests. Any time you can connect with the interviewer on common personal interests, the flow of the interview will be more relaxed.

A Personal Interests paragraph should look like this:

> **PERSONAL INTERESTS:**   Tennis and modern art.

Professional Affiliations/Associations Paragraph

The Professional Affiliations/Associations paragraph is where you would specify your membership in bar associations and/or other groups. Merely being on the mailing list of 10 professional organizations does not merit inclusion in your resume. Rather you should include professional affiliations or associations because you actively participate in them or on their behalf.

These affiliations and associations are of particular interest to law firms if they represent a positive influence on your ability to attract clients. Again, try to place yourself in the position of the employer and ask: "Why do I care if a potential new hire belongs to several associations?" The answer: This involvement shows the potential new hire is out in the community, developing contacts that may later result in clients and potential business for the law firm.

Remember, however, that membership in too many associations can make a potential law firm or corporation wary that these commitments will distract you from your practice of law making it difficult for you to commit the time they require from you.

Before deciding on including this paragraph, consider carefully whether it enhances or clutters up your resume with affiliations and associations that really have no bearing on your marketability for the position you are applying for.

A Professional Affiliations/Associations paragraph should appear like this:

PROFESSIONAL
AFFILIATIONS: Los Angeles County Bar Association (Bankruptcy Section).

Publications Paragraph

In the Publications paragraph, you can list any legal publications you have authored or co-authored. You may either include them under your Education entry or show them under the Publications paragraph.

Be sure to include the name of the article or note in quotation marks, underline the name of the legal publication, and state the date it appeared.

A Publication paragraph should look like this:

PUBLICATIONS: Authored, "The Ramifications of the Due on Sale Clause," Yale Law Journal, April 1992.

WHAT YOU SHOULD EXCLUDE

The following items are either unprofessional or inappropriate and should not appear in your resume:

- ▶ Reasons for leaving.
- ▶ Compensation requirements.
- ▶ Marital status, name of spouse, and/or names of children.
- ▶ Personal information.
- ▶ Photograph.
- ▶ Names, addresses, and phone numbers of references.
- ▶ Inappropriate personal interests.
- ▶ Job objective statement.
- ▶ Summary of qualifications.
- ▶ Significant accomplishments.
- ▶ Nonlegal employment experience.

The following sections explain why these items should be excluded.

Reasons for Leaving

You should never state your reasons for leaving your present employment in your resume or in your cover letter. You should address this subject only if you are asked about it during the interview. We will discuss how to answer this question appropriately in Chapter 4.

The reason for not including this material in your resume is that it is usually a delicate and confidential subject that can be more diplomatically handled one-on-one in a personal interview setting.

Compensation Requirements

The subject of compensation requires great sensitivity and should be delayed until the end of your interview process unless you are asked about your present compensation. Your compensation requirements should not be stated in your resume, as you may "price" yourself out of consideration. We will discuss the compensation issue in greater depth in Chapter 4.

Many large law firms in today's market already have predetermined base salaries for attorneys with two, three, or four years of practice. Such firms can only pay you what they pay other attorneys at the same level.

With smaller law firms, your compensation requirements may be equally irrelevant, as they tend to compensate new hires on a sliding scale, in line with the salaries of the other attorneys in their employ.

Corporations are, perhaps, the one entity where compensation is negotiable; however, the legal departments of some corporations are similar to smaller law firms and salaries are often dictated by budget determinations.

Compensation requirements do not belong on your resume or cover letter, but rather should become a natural consequence of the interview process and mutual interest.

Marital Status, Name of Spouse, and/or Names of Children

It is more common, than favored, for attorneys to include information on resumes about whether they are married, divorced, separated, or single, and whether they have children. Some attorneys have even gone as far as listing the family members' names. We are not antifamily, quite the contrary; however, including this data on your resume begs the question of relevance. Again, ask why the employer should consider your candidacy more favorably because you are married to Candice and have three children, Sue, age nine, Charles, age 6, and Ben, age 4. Or ask why it should matter that you are single with an 8-year-old German Shepherd named Ralph?

Again, this kind of information does not enhance your marketability as an attorney.

Personal Information

Do not include personal information about your weight, height, Social Security number, or religious or political affiliation. Again, this information is not relevant to your qualifications as an attorney.

Photograph

Never include your photograph with your resume. Whether you are attractive or not is irrelevant to your ability to practice law. Resumes with photographs have been summarily ridiculed and are never taken seriously.

Names, Addresses, and Phone Numbers of References

There are several reasons you should not list your references on your resume.

First, your references are a confidential part of your employment history. At the appropriate time, in the interview process, you will be asked to supply one or more references. At that time, you should divulge the names of your references and where they can be reached. Always obtain permission and assurance of cooperation from your intended references before releasing their names to any potential employer.

Second, if you send your resume with references' names and phone numbers to several employers, these references may be contacted several times. Such phone calls abuse the generosity of your reference providers. One glowing reference to a serious and interested potential employer will help you far more than several lukewarm references to nosy "lookey-loos" more interested in gossip than your professional career.

Third, but not to be overlooked, is that including names, addresses, and phone numbers of references takes up unnecessary space on your resume. Again, the goal is to make your one-page resume stand out. Information about references within the body of your resume only adds excess to it, not enhancement.

Inappropriate Personal Interests

If you choose to use this paragraph to show more about your activities, apart from the practice of law, think carefully about what you include. Again, remember the purpose of this paragraph. It is not about what makes you a better attorney; instead, it offers an open window on other aspects of your life. In doing so, it must not offend a potential employer.

An amusing example will highlight how such a paragraph can "turn off" a potential employer. We represented an attorney, who had everything going for him. He had graduated with high distinction from a top law school and was working for a well-respected Chicago-based law firm. His resume would certainly have been favorably received by a prospective law firm for a screening interview. In his personal interest statement, however, he noted the following: Enjoy nude modeling for *Playgirl,* sailing, and reading mysteries.

Most legal employers would deem "nude modeling" to be unprofessional and inappropriate, and so we tactfully counseled him to remove this "personal interest" from his resume.

Job Objective Statement

The job objective statement is the most overused and ineffective way to communicate your interests to a law firm or corporation. Presumably, when you send your resume to a potential employer, you are either responding to an advertisement or are contacting firms or companies that might be able to use your services. Hence, you should briefly state any reference to a sought-after position in the opening paragraph of your cover letter, not your resume.

Furthermore, you run the risk that such an explicitly stated position may not be available. Instead, another position that might be open and equally interesting may evade your grasp because your job objective statement is too narrowly drafted. To avoid this possibility, some attorneys draft their job objective statement so broadly that almost any position can become the one they are seeking.

Again, considering the importance of the space allocation of your resume, do not include anything that does not enhance or add to your marketability as a prospective new hire.

Summary of Qualifications

Your qualifications are certainly relevant to your resume; however, they should appear within the body of other appropriate sections. If your qualifications are directly related to your legal experience, then the information should appear within either the Professional Experience paragraph or the Employment History paragraph. Educational qualifications should be included within the Education paragraph.

If the information is not appropriate in those or other sections of your resume, you should consider omitting it.

Significant Accomplishments

Significant accomplishments likewise should appear within the appropriate sections of your resume. Accomplishments directly related to your legal experience should be included either within the Professional Experience paragraph or the Employment History paragraph. Significant educational achievements belong in the Education paragraph.

If the information cannot be used in those or other appropriate sections, then you should consider excluding it from your resume.

Nonlegal Employment Experience

Although nonlegal employment experience is relevant to your life experience, it may be irrelevant to the present position you seek. Your main objective, within the context of your attorney resume, should be to demonstrate to a prospective employer why you are qualified for a position as an attorney. Hence, jobs in industries outside the practice of law are unlikely to exhibit useful attributes.

There are, however, a couple of exceptions to this rule. If you are a dual degree candidate, such as a J.D./M.B.A., and have been previously employed in the corporate world utilizing your M.B.A., you should briefly state the name of your employer and describe your responsibilities. Remember, though, that your legal experience always outweighs your other experience when you are applying for a position as an attorney.

Another example of the application of this exception, is the practice of law as a second career. For example, if your first career was in the insurance industry as a property and casualty underwriter and you are now a law school graduate seeking a position as an attorney, you may briefly include your work experience in the insurance field prior to and/or during law school. It is also important to explain the presumed gap in time between your undergraduate and law school education degrees. This information has particular importance if you are interested in a related area of legal practice, such as insurance coverage litigation.

Unless your nonlegal work experience is similar to the preceding exceptions, it should not be included in your resume. The space on your resume should be reserved for only the most pertinent examples of your qualifications for a position as an attorney.

DIFFERENCES IN RESUMES FOR JUNIOR LAWYERS AND EXPERIENCED LAWYERS

Resumes of junior attorneys and senior, or more experienced, attorneys differ in content rather than in organization. In both cases, the resume should be organized as stated throughout this chapter; however, senior attorneys should stress their experience and bar association activities that directly reflect involvement in their practice area. Unlike the resume of a junior attorney, the resume of a senior attorney frequently exceeds one page. A second page is appropriate where an attorney possesses a number of years of experience and has made several job changes.

The Importance of Experience versus Education

The battle of legal employment often becomes a war over whether education or experience is ultimately more important. The general rule is that a person's academic achievements in law school and undergraduate studies are often more quantifiable than employment history and legal experience. Hence, lawyers who did well academically often receive priority in interviews and subsequent employment. Generally, employers believe that if you did well in school, you will do well on the job. While we have all marveled at law school colleagues who were at the bottom of their class and went on to achieve great success in either law practice or business, law firms and corporations nevertheless tend to look at the quantifiable educational accomplishments first.

As with all rules, there are exceptions. In some areas of practice, experience has spoken more loudly than education, particularly where the demand exceeds the supply. In the practice areas of ERISA, insurance coverage, health care, and environmental and patent law, employers historically have given more weight to experience than to education.

How Should You Describe Your Experience?

As previously detailed, you should describe your professional legal experience in a well-drafted, detailed, but concise paragraph. If you are a senior attorney who has either first chaired or second chaired a trial(s), you should detail that. If you have drafted or negotiated complex corporate, real estate, or tax transactions, you should describe them. If you have drafted and negotiated other kinds of agreements, such as entertainment, labor, or family law matters, you should include them.

If you have professional experience in more than one practice area, you can still describe it in the Professional Experience paragraph, leaving one line of space between each practice area. Here is an example:

PROFESSIONAL
EXPERIENCE: **Environmental:** Includes assisting clients on such diverse matters as arranger and transporter liability in EPA Superfund sites, successor and parent corporations' liability for remediation costs, evaluation of contracts for indemnification of response costs, evaluation of insurance coverage for response costs, and impact of certain environmental statutes in condemnation proceedings.

Real Estate and Land Use: Includes drafting and negotiation of contracts for sale of contaminated commercial property and proposed purchase of property by National Parks Service, assisting clients on various zoning matters and on environmental issues related to purchase and sale transactions.

Business Litigation: Includes involvement in every aspect of complex securities fraud matters, including drafting of pleadings, discovery requests and responses, and deposing key witnesses.

Keep in mind that your Professional Experience paragraph is important. Try to include all your pertinent and significant legal accomplishments. The resume, however, is a marketing tool, so include only those accomplishments that directly relate to the job you are applying for. For example, if you are applying for a law firm position, your Professional Experience paragraph should be focused in the area of practice the firm is seeking. However, if you are applying for a general legal position, as is often the case with corporations, then feel free to be more liberal in showing the broad range of experience you possess in the Professional Experience paragraph.

SUGGESTIONS FOR OVERLAPPING PRACTICE AREAS

If you practice law in two (or more) interrelated areas, include both areas of practice within your Professional Experience or Employment History paragraph. For example, if you practice both ERISA and employee benefits law, you should combine them in discussing your legal experience. Another example might be the practice of corporate and real estate law. Although these are distinct areas of practice, they often cross over, so you should combine them in discussing your legal experience.

However, if you have experience in environmental compliance and real estate development law, you should separate these areas within the body of your Professional Experience paragraph. Even though those areas have some connection to each other, the practice areas are different enough to justify individual entries. Please refer to this Chapter, under the subhead "How Should You Describe Your Experience?" for examples of ways to handle the overlapping practice situation.

Do You Really Need a Two- or Three-Page Resume?

Just because you have a great deal of experience or are a senior attorney does not automatically mean your resume should be two or three pages long. The determining factor should be how much you need to describe. If you are a senior attorney and can still organize your resume on one page, you should do so. There is no inherent advantage in a two- or three-page resume. The sole reason for using a second or third page should be necessity, not creativity. Again, brevity is preferable.

In general, legal employers are more accepting of two-page resumes from prospective senior attorneys seeking new employment. Such employers readily understand that experienced potential job candidates may require a second page to properly detail their experience.

The basic goal, whether you are a junior attorney, senior attorney, or general counsel, is to create a concise, yet detailed resume that includes only information germane to the position you seek—no more, no less.

3

Cover Letters— General Information and Guidelines

In presenting your resume to a potential employer, do not overlook the importance of an impressive, well-polished cover letter. Even though this letter usually reiterates what is detailed in your resume, it acts as a personal dialogue between you and the prospective employer.

You should always direct your letter by name (not by title or hiring role) to an individual in the law firm or corporation. If you do not know the name of the appropriate contact, you can usually obtain this information with a mere phone call to the firm. If you are responding to an advertisement that indicates you should send your resume to the Recruiting Coordinator or Hiring Partner, you should call to get the person's name and send the letter to him or her personally, rather than to that title.

If you are responding to a blind box advertisement (one that does not reveal the name of the employer), send the letter as requested or address it: "To whom it may concern." Never assume that the hiring person is a man ("Dear Sir"); also, sending out a cover letter addressed to "Dear Sir or Madam" gives the impression of an assembly-line mail blitz.

There are three things to consider when answering a blind box ad: (1) You may be sending it unknowingly to your present employer; (2) you have no way to assertively follow up on the status of your resume; and (3) your request to keep your inquiry in confidence may not be honored, and you have no recourse should it happen. We are not discouraging you from sending your resume out to this kind of advertised position; however, please recognize the inherent risks and disadvantages.

ELEMENTS OF THE COVER LETTER

The cover letter should be formal without being stilted. Humor or sidebar rhetoric is inappropriate and unprofessional. The cover letter should be no more than one page and should include several short paragraphs. You should use well-structured, grammatical sentences that highlight what is detailed in your resume. The only new material will explain how you learned of the position available and will add that you look forward to meeting them. Let's take each paragraph, one by one, to demonstrate the format that we have used successfully for our attorney candidates.

The first paragraph of your cover letter should be limited to a few short sentences. It introduces yourself as an attorney interested in the position the law firm or corporation is offering. It should also indicate how you learned of the position. If you are answering an advertisement, state that. If you are writing at the suggestion of a member of their firm or corporation, you should state the referent's name. You should also provide a copy of your letter to the person whose suggestion you are acting on. If, on the other hand, you are sending out multiple unsolicited resumes, you should acknowledge that you are aware they may not have a current need; however, you are sending the resume in case their hiring needs should change.

The second paragraph should briefly outline your educational achievements both at the college/university and law school level. You should note your class rank here, particularly if you graduated in the top 25% of your law school class. If your law school does not rank its law students, then you should mention that. In some instances, you may want to indicate that you are including your transcripts for their review. Any law review, moot court, honors, awards, or publications should be indicated.

The third paragraph should briefly state your legal employment history with particular emphasis on your achievements at your present employer. You should indicate, if appropriate, what your current annual billing hours were for the past calendar year. If you are a litigation associate, indicate the kinds of responsibility you have attained. If you are a transactional attorney, briefly describe and quantify the depth of your involvement with large transactions. Under no circumstances should you give the names of your clients. Simply refer to them as "the firm's client," or "my client."

You can use the fourth paragraph in a variety of ways, such as to briefly state why you believe you would be an asset to their law firm or corporation. Or, if you have an established client base with what is called a "book of business," you should indicate that.

The last paragraph should only be a sentence or two. You should indicate—if this is the case—that you would appreciate them keeping your interest in confidence. This is particularly important if you are presently employed. Although all employment inquiries are confidential, your request puts the potential employer on notice that you are especially concerned about it. The last sentence should indicate that you look forward to a response at their earliest convenience.

Several sample cover letters follow. Even though each letter has a different focus, the format, for the most part, is consistent. Two cover letters, however, use a different, abbreviated format: the direct mail search to Governmental Agencies and the Court Clerkships inquiry. As you will see in the examples, they have no third or fourth paragraph as previously described. However, if you are applying for a governmental position or court clerkship and you have pertinent and relevant employment experience, then you would include it in the appropriate place within the body of the cover letter.

The format of the Networking cover letter is abbreviated as well. Here, the purpose is not to sell yourself to a prospective employer, but rather to acquire useful contacts or to "network" yourself into an opportunity for an informal discussion about potential openings.

If you have been laid off or fired, you will find additional helpful information in the section "Cover Letters for Attorneys Who Have Been Laid Off or Fired." It provides specific advice for handling this delicate situation.

Newspaper Advertisements (Direct Mail Search to Law Firms)

Suzanne C. Miller
521 West Poinsettia Street
Culver City, California 90035

September 15, 1992

Ms. Carolyne Bradford
Recruiting Coordinator
O'Melveny & Myers
333 Grand Avenue
Los Angeles, California 90010

Dear Ms. Bradford:

In response to your advertisement for a mid-level corporate securities associate in last week's Los Angeles Daily Journal, enclosed please find my resume.

In 1988, I graduated Order of the Coif from the U.C.L.A. School of Law. During my first year of law school, I received two American Jurisprudence Awards, one in Real Property and the other in Civil Procedure. I graduated *summa cum laude* with a Bachelor of Arts degree in Economics from U.C.L.A. in 1985.

Since graduation from U.C.L.A. School of Law, I have been associated with Skadden, Arps, Slate, Meagher & Flom, where I have been involved in a sophisticated corporate securities practice.

In spite of the market fluctuations in the corporate practice area, I have consistently billed 2400 hours annually. While many of my clients have been long-standing Skadden clients, I have generated some new business on my own. I am confident they would follow me wherever I practice.

Please keep this inquiry in strict confidence. Thank you for your consideration. I look forward to hearing from you.

Sincerely,

Suzanne C. Miller

SCM/me
Enclosure

Newspaper Advertisements (Direct Mail Search to Corporations)

Robert James Cackleburn
1222 Eureka Place
Washington, DC 20036

January 25, 1993

Mr. Roger Beckton
Manager, Human Resources
Atlantic Richfield Company
P.O. Box 77756
Los Angeles, California 90071

Dear Mr. Beckton:

In response to your advertisement for a junior environmental litigation attorney in yesterday's <u>Wall Street Journal</u>, enclosed please find my resume.

In 1990, I graduated from Harvard University Law School, where I was Editor in Chief of the <u>Harvard Law Review</u>. Prior to that, I graduated from Stanford University with a Bachelor of Arts degree in History, where I maintained a 4.0 grade-point average.

Since graduation from Harvard, I have been associated with Arnold & Porter in their Washington, DC office. While I believe I have received good training and experience, I am interested in practicing environmental law in-house with a well-respected corporation such as yours.

I am seriously interested in relocating to Los Angeles, and I am already registered to take the February California bar exam. If you are interested in meeting with me, perhaps we could schedule an interview at that time.

Please keep this inquiry in strict confidence. Thank you for your consideration. I look forward to hearing from you.

Sincerely,

Robert James Cackleburn

RJC/ me
Enclosure

Newspaper Advertisements (Blind Box Ads)

Samuel R. Prestone
3221 Cadillac Avenue
Chicago, Illinois 60605

March 26, 1993

Box 347898
The Chicago Tribune
Chicago, Illinois 60606

To whom it may concern:

In response to your advertisement for a mid-level commercial litigation associate in last week's The Chicago Tribune, enclosed please find my resume.

In 1989, I graduated in the Top 6% of my class from Georgetown University Law Center. During my third year of law school, I received an American Jurisprudence Award for International Tax. Prior to that, I graduated from the University of Michigan in 1986 with a Bachelor of Arts degree with high distinction in Economics.

Presently, I am associated with Mayer, Brown & Platt, where I am involved with sophisticated financial institution clients. I have been involved in the whole range of pretrial and discovery matters, as well as having drafted complex negotiation agreements.

I am particularly interested in the litigation position you are advertising because it would offer me an opportunity to develop actual trial experience. I feel that such a position would enhance my career as a litigation attorney.

Please keep this inquiry in strict confidence. Thank you for your consideration. I look forward to hearing from you.

Sincerely,

Samuel R. Prestone

SRP/ me
Enclosure

Direct Mail Search to Governmental Agencies

Sandra Sullivan
333 North Palm Drive, Apt. No. 205
Beverly Hills, California 90210

January 10, 1987

Ursula Rathbone, Esq.
U.S. Attorney's Office
Central District of California
312 North Spring Street
Los Angeles, California 90012

Dear Ms. Rathbone:

I am writing to you to apply for the position as an Assistant U.S. Attorney. I am interested in the office because I would like to acquire trial experience.

In 1987, I graduated from Yale University Law School, where I served as Note and Comment Editor of the Yale Law Review. In 1985, I graduated with honors from Catholic University with a Bachelor of Science degree in Accounting.

Since graduation, I have been associated with the Los Angeles office of White & Case. While I have received excellent training in their litigation department, I feel that an opportunity to further develop my trial experience would be beneficial. I believe that only within the U.S. Attorney's Office will I acquire the skills I am interested in developing.

Please keep this inquiry in strict confidence. Thank you for your consideration. I look forward to hearing from you.

Sincerely,

Sandra Sullivan

SS/me
Enclosure

Direct Mail Search to Court Clerkships

Sandra Sullivan
1758 Whaler Road
New Haven, Connecticut 06509

January 3, 1984

The Honorable Robert Smith, Associate Justice
United States District Court for the Central District of California
312 North Spring Street
Los Angeles, California 90012

Re: Judicial Clerkship for 1985-86 Term

Dear Judge Smith:

I am writing to you to apply for the position as your law clerk during the 1985-86 term. I would like to clerk for you because I enjoy writing and am interested in working in an environment where the interpretations of law are debated and decided.

As you will see from the enclosed resume, I am currently a third year law student at Yale University Law School. I serve as the Note and Comment Editor of the <u>Yale Law Review,</u> and my article "The Constitutional Rights of the Homeless" is scheduled for publication in the Fall 1985 issue of the <u>Review</u>. I have enclosed a copy of my most recent draft of the article for your review and consideration. I have also enclosed a copy of my law school transcript.

While I am presently attending law school in Connecticut, I can fly into Los Angeles, where my parents reside, to interview at your convenience. I look forward to hearing from you.

Sincerely,

Sandra Sullivan

SS/me
Enclosures

Legal Search Firm and/or Executive Recruiter

Tanya Rappaport
193 Manhole Avenue, Apt. No. 4
San Francisco, California 94014

April 10, 1993

Mary Jo Russo
Russo & Fondell
9348 Civic Center Drive, Suite 101
Beverly Hills, California 90210

Dear Ms. Russo:

Charlie Keystone, a former colleague of mine, recommended you as someone who could help me find an in-house position. Charlie said that you helped him find a great job with Sanwa Bank in their in-house legal department. I am interested in something similar to that. I would be interested in either Northern or Southern California opportunities.

Enclosed is my current resume indicating my real estate development experience. I have been associated with Landels, Ripley & Diamond since law school graduation in 1988. I've received extensive training and experience. However, as I become more senior and partnership becomes a looming possibility, I recognize that frankly I'm not suited for the "partnership/book of business" stress. Hence, I am interested in finding employment either with a real estate developer or with a financial institution's real estate department.

In addition to my law degree from Hastings College of Law, I have earned an M.B.A. from the University of California, at Berkeley. I feel that both of these degrees enhance my capabilities as an attorney and as a businesswoman.

Please contact me at my office, but do not leave a message with my secretary. No one at the firm knows that I am considering a job change. Feel free to leave a message on my voice mail, as it is private. I look forward to hearing from you.

Sincerely,

Tanya Rappaport

TR/me
Enclosure

Networking

Stephen Baret
4770 Main Street
Venice, California 92272
(310) 398-7271

March 4, 1993

Craig Patterson, Esq.
Fox Studios
9366 Sunset Boulevard
Hollywood, California 90035

Dear Craig:

It was great running into you at Jane's birthday party last weekend. I haven't seen you since law school graduation. I was happy to hear that you're enjoying practicing law at Fox Studios.

Although we discussed it only briefly, I would like to learn more about your position. Just recently, I've decided to make a move myself and am interested in learning more about practicing in-house with a studio.

I would enjoy taking you out to lunch so we can catch up on what's happening. How does next Friday for lunch around 1:00 sound to you? You pick the place. Please call me at my home phone number above to confirm. I look forward to seeing you.

Sincerely,

Stephen Baret

SB/me

Referral Letter

Carolyn Rigoletto
4770 Main Street
Austin, Texas 73343

February 15, 1993

Paul Pachuleski, Esq.
Andrews & Kurth
4200 Texas Commerce Tower
Houston, Texas 77002

Dear Mr. Pachuleski:

Dirk Brian, of your Dallas office, suggested I send you my resume. He mentioned that your Houston office has a position open for a labor associate at my level. Dirk and I attended the University of Texas School of Law and have remained in contact since. He speaks very highly of you and the firm.

In 1987, I graduated Top 13% from the University of Texas, at Austin. In 1984, I graduated *cum laude* with a Bachelor of Science degree in Broadcasting and Film from Boston University.

Since graduation, I have been associated with Blazier, Rutland & Lerner in Austin, where I have practiced labor and employment law. Your labor practice, as described by Dirk, is similar to that of Blazier et al.

I am sincerely interested in hearing more about your firm's labor position and look forward to hearing from you. Please keep this inquiry in strict confidence. Thank you for your consideration.

Sincerely,

Carolyn Rigoletto

CR/me
Enclosure

COVER LETTERS FOR ATTORNEYS WHO HAVE BEEN LAID OFF OR FIRED

In years past, being laid off or fired could and did wreak havoc on an attorney's career. While this situation can present difficulties, attorneys have learned to deal with layoffs and firings in new ways. Rather than hide the fact from a potential employer, attorneys are being straightforward and honest about this matter.

In the examples that follow, we will demonstrate how to handle terminations within the context of a cover letter. You can and should deal with the subject briefly and matter-of-factly. By addressing it at the outset, you can overcome the difficulty of having to deal with it during an interview.

You can address the issue of being laid off or fired in the first paragraph (where you have stated how you learned of the position and why you are looking for a new position), in the third paragraph (where you briefly discuss your present employment situation), or in the fourth paragraph (where you indicate your interest in the position offered).

If you have been laid off or fired, you may include the name and phone number of a reference provider within your cover letter, assuming you have been granted permission to do so. Since finding employment can be more difficult if you have been laid off or fired, providing a reference gives a potential employer the opportunity to inquire into the matter, thereby assuaging any concern he or she may have.

The following samples should assist you in handling the delicate circumstance of being laid off or fired.

Cover Letter if Laid Off

Linda Sacks
1804 Ridpath Drive
Los Angeles, California 90048

November 13, 1992

Prescilla Westman, Esq.
Manatt, Phelps, & Phillips
11355 West Olympic Boulevard
Los Angeles, California 90048

Dear Ms. Westman:

Paul Walters, of your firm, suggested I send you my resume. He mentioned that your firm has a position open for a third-year healthcare associate. Unfortunately, I was recently informed that I am among several associates in my department who are being asked to leave. The reasons given for the layoffs were economic. I have been assured that I will receive good references.

In 1989, I graduated Top 15% from the Temple University School of Law, where I was a member of the Temple Law Review. Prior to that, I received my Bachelor of Science degree in Public Health and Economics in 1986 from the University of California at San Diego, where I maintained a 3.9 grade-point average.

Since graduation, I have been associated with Weissburg & Aronson in their Los Angeles office. I am involved in varied aspects of health care law. While at the firm, I have taken on a great deal of responsibility.

Given the circumstances surrounding my employment, I am prepared to offer you the name and phone number of my reference. Her name is Nancy O'Callack, Esq. She is the supervising Partner in my department. She can be reached at (310) 273-7687. Please feel free to contact her, if you have serious interest.

Thank you for your consideration. I look forward to hearing from you.

Sincerely,

Linda Sacks

LS/me
Enclosure

Cover Letter if Laid Off

Richard Voss
8746 MacArthur Court
Newport Beach, California 92660

December 18, 1993

Mr. Bart Spencer
Human Resource Department
Collagen Corporation
2500 Faber Place,
Dept. SPD
Palo Alto, California 94303

Dear Mr. Spencer:

In response to your advertisement for an Associate Patent Counsel position in yesterday's Wall Street Journal, enclosed please find my resume. I was recently informed that my legal position at ATV Systems will be eliminated due to budget cutbacks. Hence, I am interested in exploring an opportunity with your company.

In 1987, I graduated Order of the Coif from Loyola Marymount University Law School in Los Angeles, where I was a Member of the Loyola Law Review. Prior to that, I received a B.S.E.E. in 1984, from the University of California at Los Angeles.

At graduation and until December 1988, I was associated with the law firm of Lyon & Lyon in Los Angeles, where I prepared and assisted in the preparation and prosecution of patent and trademark applications. I was recruited by ATV Systems in Anaheim, to join their patent department and was promoted within the department to Assistant Patent Counsel. I have supervised ten senior patent attorneys in all patent licensing matters.

Given my present employment situation, I am prepared to give you the name of the person who can provide you with an excellent reference. Thank you for your consideration. I look forward to hearing from you.

Sincerely,

Richard Voss

RV/me
Enclosure

Cover Letter if Fired

Kathryn Sutton
1623 North 24th Street
Phoenix, Arizona 85004

September 15, 1993

Patrick Carroway, Esq.
Snell & Wilmer
3100 Valley Bank Center
Phoenix, Arizona 85018

Dear Mr. Carroway:

In response to your advertisement for a senior estate planning and probate associate in yesterday's Wall Street Journal, enclosed please find my resume.

In 1986, I graduated Top 10% from the University of Arizona College of Law. I graduated in 1983 from Arizona State University with a Bachelor of Arts degree in English, where I maintained a 3.8 grade-point average.

Since January 1989, I have been associated with Brown & Bain in Phoenix. I have practiced within their estate planning and probate department. There, I have drafted several kinds of trust instruments, as well as represented and negotiated complicated estate tax audits on behalf of my clients. I have also provided my clients with sophisticated estate tax planning advice. My current position has recently been terminated, and my last day at the firm will be October 15, 1993.

Thank you for your serious consideration. If you are interested in my references and/or any other further information, please do not hesitate to contact me.

Sincerely,

Kathryn Sutton

KS/me
Enclosure

Cover Letter if Fired

Stanton Leach
5786 Mammoth Avenue, Apt. No. 450
Denver, Colorado 80206

April 25, 1993

Marcus Shatuck, Esq.
General Counsel
Blue Cross & Blue Shield of Colorado
700 Broadway
Denver, Colorado 80112

Dear Mr. Shatuck:

Although you may not have a current position available in the areas of ERISA and employee benefits, enclosed please find my resume.

In 1988, I graduated Top 15% from Seton Hall University School of Law. In 1985, I graduated with a Bachelor of Arts degree in Economics from Colorado College.

Since March 1989, I have acted as Vice President of Compensation and Benefits Compliance for the Porter Memorial Hospital in Denver. I have been involved in all legal aspects of compensation, welfare benefit, and pension plans. I have directly interfaced with the I.R.S., Department of Labor, and the Security Exchange Commission, as well as other regulatory agencies. Prior to this position, I was a tax law specialist with the I.R.S. in Trenton, New Jersey.

My employment with the hospital has been terminated. In the event a position should become available, I would welcome the opportunity to meet with you. Thank you for your consideration.

Sincerely,

Stanton Leach

SL/me
Enclosure

KEEPING ACCURATE RECORDS OF YOUR CORRESPONDENCE AND RESUME

It is not only advisable but necessary to record all your correspondence in an orderly fashion. Your records should indicate the following:

1. The date of your correspondence.
2. To whom the letter and resume was sent.
3. To which law firm or corporation you sent it.
4. Date of first response from prospective employer.
5. Rejection or invitation to interview.
6. Date and name of person(s) met on 1st interview.
7. Date of thank-you note(s).
8. Date and name of person(s) met on 2nd interview.
9. Date of thank-you note(s).
10. Date and name of person(s) met on 3rd interview.
11. Date of thank-you note(s).

Having such a file system will make your job search process much easier and more organized. In addition to this job search worksheet, you should have a duplicate copy of all correspondence.

Date	
Contact person	
Law Firm or Corp	
Response Date	
Rejection	
Date & Name of Person met on 1st Interview	
Thank you note date 1	
Date & Name of Person met on 2nd Interview	
Thank you note date 2	
Date & Name of Person met on 3rd Interview	
Thank you note date 3	
Personal Comments and Impressions	

4

Landing the Screening Interview

Congratulations! You have received a call from a prospective legal employer inviting you to come in for a screening interview. Let's discuss its purpose and focus.

The screening interview is about chemistry, that is, the chemistry between you and your interviewer. While there is no guarantee that you will "click" with everyone you meet, we can give you some suggestions that will put you at ease and help you have a successful screening interview:

1. After the firm or corporation notifies you of its interest, set the interview up promptly.
2. Choose your interview attire carefully.
3. Be prepared for your interview.
4. Learn how to handle questions related to why you are considering an employment change.

THE BASICS OF SETTING UP THE INITIAL INTERVIEW

While this procedure might seem obvious, you would be surprised at the various ways in which initial screening interviews are scheduled. First, you should promptly return the phone call to the person who called you or whomever you have been directed to contact. "Promptly" means that you should return the call that day or the following morning. Delaying your return call can project a poor image of your sincere interest.

Even though your schedule may be busy with court dates or deadline transactions, you should set up an interview as soon as the interviewer can meet with you. Timing is everything. Flow with the energy created by their interest in you. Do not sandwich this interview between two other matters. Allow enough time to arrive at your interview and for the possibility that your interviewer may be running late, as well as for the positive potential that your interview may go over the usual 45-minute duration.

Interviewing is an emotional dynamic, and timing, energy, and flow are what push an interview to its successful conclusion.

WHAT SHOULD YOU WEAR?

This section is not a "dress for success" manual; however, first impressions are important. Just as your resume provided the first impression of you as an attorney, your personal appearance needs to complement your resume.

While the legal profession has changed greatly in the past several decades, it remains one of the last bastions of conservatism. Therefore, whether you are male or female, you should dress professionally in a business suit. Dark conservative colors, such as navy, gray, charcoal, and black are usually preferred. Avoid bright, loud colors that distract from the purpose of the interview. Even though members of the law firm or corporation you are interviewing with might wear more casual attire, remember that you are on an interview, which always tends to be more formal.

Generally speaking, you should err on the conservative side when dressing for your interview.

PREPARING FOR THE INTERVIEW

This initial interview is too important to just let happen. Therefore, prior to your meeting, you should prepare for it. Your preparation need not be complicated, but you should do it thoroughly. Though much of the interview is chemistry, you will want to be fairly informed about your potential employer. Several sources of information are available to you, some more accessible than others.

For information about a prospective law firm, try the following resources:

1. *The Martindale-Hubbell Law Directory of Lawyers* (Reed Publishing). Simply look in the directory of the state and city of

the law firm. Locate the listing for the firm. The firm will list the areas of practice as well as the names of its attorneys, both partners and associates, with a biography of each attorney. It is also helpful to inquire, at the time you schedule your interview, whom you will be meeting on your interview, so you can be better prepared about the background(s) of your interviewer(s). Another suggestion is to check the law firm's Martindale-Hubbell listing to see if there is anyone from your law school or any friend who might be able to provide you with some information on the interview style of your interviewer.

2. *A Law Firm Resume.* This resume, or profile, prepared by the law firm often highlights the areas of practice as well as the industries of its clients. It also often profiles partners and associates. When you set up your interview, ask your contact to send you a copy of an updated firm resume.

3. *The National Association for Law Placement (NALP).* This organization produces an annual *Directory of Legal Employers* as a companion to NALPLINE, available through WESTLAW. The directory indicates an employer's hiring characteristics and practices. While the audience focus is law school students, it still provides valuable factual information, not available in the *Martindale-Hubbell* or the law firm's resume.

4. *The American Lawyer.* This magazine produces an annual supplement called "The Am Law 100," which lists the gross revenues and net profits of the highest grossing firms in the United States. This magazine also publishes an annual summer associates' survey that rates the law firms on the basis of training, billable hours, compensation, and the like.

If you are interested in finding information regarding a prospective corporation, the following should be helpful:

1. *Law & Business: Directory of Corporate Counsel* (Prentice-Hall Law & Business). This is a comprehensive guide to the organization and personnel of corporate and nonprofit law departments.

2. *Martindale-Hubbell Law Directory* (Reed Publishing). Within this directory, there is a section on Corporate Law departments. The biography of each attorney is listed within each corporation.

3. *A Corporation's Annual Report.* Most corporations produce an annual report. At the time you set up an interview, ask your contact to send you a copy of the most recent annual report, organizational chart, and any other information that would be helpful.

HANDLING A TOUGH QUESTION—WHY ARE YOU CONSIDERING AN EMPLOYMENT CHANGE?

The interview process is like a layer cake, in that the interviewer seeks to ascertain more about you by assembling answers to layers of questions. Your interviewer will ask different kinds of questions to determine whether you are a strong candidate and then will ask you to return for a round of further interviews (referred to as "callback" interviews). Some questions will be routine and easy, while others will be complex and difficult to answer. Diplomacy and tactfulness are required in dealing with these difficult questions.

Let's examine one difficult question that arises during an interview and discuss how to handle it. The following question potentially exposes a myriad of possible responses. Before we can direct you on how to respond, we must first know the *real* reasons behind your decision to make a change. A list of the common reasons are listed after the question.

Why are you considering leaving your present employer?

1. Personality conflicts.
2. Nonexistent or inadequate training.
3. Below-market compensation.
4. Unreasonable billable hour requirements.
5. Not getting the kind of work you want.
6. Laid off or fired.
7. Long commute to work.
8. "Passed over" for partnership.

Personality Conflicts

Personality conflicts are common reasons people desire job changes. While many of us have experienced this difficulty and are understanding about it, there are better ways of handling this matter than sharing your anger with a sympathetic ear. During your interview, never "bad mouth" your employer or anyone at your present place of employment. The only safe policy is to avoid mentioning personality conflicts as a reason for your decision to leave your job.

Nonexistent or Inadequate Training

Assume you are a first-year corporate associate working for an 80 attorney law firm. You have to handle most of your assignments with little or no direction. After you have completed your work, your supervising Partner often advises you that it is inadequate and requests that you redo it but does not offer any further guidance. After many such occurrences, you have decided to search for a position that provides better training.

Or, you might have received the impression that your law firm would routinely conduct training sessions for its junior associates or would pay for continuing education through bar courses. However, you learn that this is not the case.

Training is an important part of a young attorney's career. The economic circumstances today prevent many employers from providing the kind of training they have offered in the past. Often, this lack of training options is the reason junior associates explore other opportunities.

If you are asked why you are leaving your present employment and your reason is the desire for better training, you should answer this question honestly. Keep in mind, however, that when you answer the preceding question with "inadequate training," you may raise doubts about whether the training you have, in fact, received will satisfy the prospective employer's needs. Nevertheless, it is always preferable to acknowledge this issue up front. Otherwise, you may not be able to fulfill the employer's expectations once you have been hired.

Below-Market Compensation

You may learn, for example, from a law school classmate that she is earning $8,000 more per year than you. The law firm she works for is in the same city, has a similar practice, and is approximately the same size as the firm you work for. Or, you may be employed with a small local law firm and learn that attorneys at larger law firms work the same number of hours but earn substantially more money.

As a general rule, your sole reason for seeking another position should not be the compensation issue. While the desire to earn more money is a legitimate one, you should not communicate that goal as the reason for leaving your present position. You need to have other reasons for pursuing employment opportunities. Discuss those reasons instead.

Unreasonable Billable Hour Requirement

Assume you are working at a law firm that insists on a requirement of 2,100 billable hours excluding any pro bono or firm administrative time. While you are adequately and fairly compensated, the demands of the billable-hour requirement do not permit you any time for outside activities. So you decide to search for a law firm position with a lower billable hour requirement or to investigate an in-house opportunity.

You must handle this subject as delicately as the subject of compensation. We understand how an employer's billable hour requirement can consume the other parts of your life, often leaving little time for friends and family. However, during an interview, if you are asked why you are leaving your present employer, you may not want to emphasize that the firm's work demands were excessive. Few potential employers would welcome hearing that you want to work less hours for them.

Not Getting the Kind of Work You Want

This answer does not usually pose problems. Simply stated, you can tell the interviewer that you are considering other employment because you are interested in another area of practice or are not getting the kind of responsibility you feel you can handle. This goal does not negatively reflect on the law firm or corporation you presently work for; rather, it is a function of your personal desire and preference.

Actually, this reason allows you to discuss the kinds of work you would like to do. Hence, it opens up new avenues of discussion for you and your interviewer. However, first research the potential employer's practice needs and ascertain that it offers such opportunities. For example, if you are a litigation associate and want to expand your practice to include entertainment litigation, then you should make sure that the prospective employer is involved in that area.

Laid Off or Fired

In a typical scenario, you are an attorney within a corporate legal department. As a result of your company's acquisition by another company, a reduction in staff has eliminated your position. You've been given 30 days' notice and have been told you will receive good references. In this situation, you should have no hesitation in openly discussing the circumstances.

If you are an attorney who has been fired for poor work product, failure to meet deadlines, or personal reasons, you may have difficulty receiving a positive reference; in such a situation, you must handle the facts with diplomacy.

Honesty is the best policy. As discussed in Chapter 3, you should have already indicated to a potential employer that you have either been laid off or fired. Therefore, when you arrive at the scheduled interview, you should not have to reveal this as new information. However, if you failed to include it in your cover letter, you should briefly explain that you were laid off or fired and briefly explain the circumstances. For the past few years, law firms and corporations have made and continue to make economic decisions to reduce their staff. As a result, being laid off or fired is not an uncommon reason, nor is it as difficult to overcome as in the past. To omit this fact can and will backfire on you.

Long Commute to Work

This is a familiar reason, particularly for attorneys who live and work in large metropolitan areas, such as Los Angeles, San Francisco, and New York. While finding employment closer to home may be a legitimate personal concern, most employers would not find this an adequate reason to exchange one job for another. Therefore, consider other reasons for making a job change, and discuss those reasons instead.

"Passed Over" for Partnership

This reason has become a truism. In years past, partnership was granted fairly automatically to those who were loyal to their law firm and who maintained association for six to seven years. In the recent past, however, law firm partnerships have altered in duration, as well as in scope. Today, law firms have extended their partnership track to as many as 10 years, and their policies are dictated by bottom-line economics.

As a result, firms are rethinking the old adage of loyalty and association. The prevalent new belief is that business, clients, and money make a firm strong and economically fit. Therefore, associates are finding that they have to be as talented at getting clients as they are at practicing law. The demands of the legal profession have changed dramatically, leaving many associates passed over for partnership.

This reason is legitimate and should be discussed openly at an interview, but you must do so without making disparaging comments about your present employer.

5

The Thank-You Letter and the Callback Interview

The thank-you letter is an often overlooked part of the interview process. This thoughtful, personal touch reminds the interviewer of your genuine interest in the position being offered. You should send a handwritten or typewritten thank-you note to your interviewer as soon as possible after your meeting. If you met with several people, you should write individual notes to them. While the letter can be concise, you should express your appreciation for the invitation to learn more about the firm or corporation and indicate that you would welcome the opportunity to meet with them again.

EXAMPLES OF THANK-YOU LETTERS

The following examples include thank-you letters following screening and callback interviews at various employment circumstances as well as thank-you letters following interviews at a governmental agency and a court clerkship.

Letter Following the Screening Interview at a Corporation

Robert James Cackleburn, Esq.
1222 Eureka Place
Washington, DC 20036

March 1, 1993

Mr. Roger Beckton
Manager, Human Resources
Atlantic Richfield Company
P.O. Box 77756
Los Angeles, California 90071

Dear Mr. Beckton:

It was a pleasure meeting with you last week. I enjoyed learning more about your company's legal department.

I feel my environmental legal experience at Arnold & Porter is similar to your environmental practice in-house. I would be interested in discussing the job position further with you. I will be in Los Angeles, again, in three weeks and would be pleased to extend my trip to meet with you and your company staff.

As we discussed, I will send two writing samples to your attention later this week. I look forward to hearing from you.

Please contact me if you need further information. Thank you for your consideration.

Sincerely,

Robert James Cackleburn

RJC/xx

Letter Following the Screening Interview at a Law Firm

Suzanne C. Miller
521 West Poinsettia Street
Culver City, California 90035

October 12, 1992

Barry Trokman, Esq.
O'Melveny & Myers
333 Grand Avenue
Los Angeles, California 90010

Dear Mr. Trokman:

It was a pleasure meeting with you earlier this week. I enjoyed hearing about your firm's corporate practice and its long-term goals.

I feel my corporate securities experience would blend nicely with your firm's practice. I am also confident that my corporate clients would benefit by your firm's sophisticated tax practice.

Please contact me if you need further information or would like to set up another interview. I look forward to hearing from you.

Sincerely,

Suzanne C. Miller

SCM/vv

Letter Following the Callback Interview at a Corporation

Tanya Rappaport
193 Manhole Avenue, Apt. No. 4
San Francisco, California 94104

June 24, 1993

Theodore Cranston, Esq.
Wells Fargo Bank, N.A.
111 Sutter Street, 20th Floor
San Francisco, California 94163

Dear Ted:

It was a pleasure meeting with you and Walter Rauscher yesterday. I enjoyed learning more about your real estate finance practice. Even though most of my legal experience has been in the real estate development area, I am interested in your bank's finance practice. I welcome the opportunity to learn more about your practice needs.

I am sorry that Dexter Swenson was unable to join us at lunch. I hope that I will be able to meet him in the near future.

Please contact me if you need further information. Thank you for your consideration.

Sincerely,

Tanya Rappaport

TA/cv

Letter Following the Callback Interview at a Law Firm

Samuel R. Prestone
3221 Cadillac Avenue
Chicago, Illinois 60605

April 19, 1993

Franklin Popover, Esq.
Sonnenschein, Nath & Rosenthal
Suite 8888, Sears Tower
233 South Wacker Drive
Chicago, Illinois 60606

Dear Frank:

Thank you so much for introducing me to your Litigation department. Meeting your Litigation partners and associates provided me with ample opportunity to realize the depth of experience your firm possesses.

In particular, I enjoyed meeting Craig Courtwright and Prescilla Easterbrook over lunch. Their vast trial experience was very impressive.

Needless to say, I am genuinely interested in your firm and your litigation department. I would welcome the opportunity to join your firm.

I look forward to hearing from you. Thank you for your consideration.

Sincerely,

Samuel R. Prestone

SRP/mm

Letter Following the Interview at a Governmental Agency

Sandra Sullivan
333 North Palm Drive, Apt. No. 205
Beverly Hills, California 90210

February 5, 1987

Ursula Rathbone, Esq.
U.S. Attorney's Office
Central District of California
312 North Spring Street
Los Angeles, California 90012

Dear Ursula:

It was a pleasure meeting with you yesterday. I enjoyed learning more about the U.S. Attorney's office.

I am enthusiastic about the prospect of joining the U.S. Attorney's office. I feel it would further enhance my skills as a litigator.

As we discussed, I will send two writing samples to your attention later this week. I look forward to hearing from you.

Please contact me if you need further information. Thank you for your consideration.

Sincerely,

Sandra Sullivan

SS/me

Letter Following the Interview for a Court Clerkship

Sandra Sullivan
1759 Whaler Road
New Haven, Connecticut 06509

February 20, 1984

The Honorable Robert Smith, Associate Judge
United States District Court for the Central District of California
312 North Spring Street
Los Angeles, California 90012

Dear Judge Smith:

It was a pleasure meeting with you last week. I enjoyed learning more about the way the Court works and specifically about the duties of a Law Clerk.

I am very interested in the position of Law Clerk for the 1985-86 term. I am pleased that you enjoyed my article, "The Constitutional Rights of the Homeless" and that you have expressed an interest in reading other articles I have written. Enclosed is an article I wrote recently, "The Constitutional Rights of Refugees Seeking Political Asylum."

Please contact me if you need further information. I am prepared to make myself available for further interviews. I look forward to hearing from you.

Sincerely,

Sandra Sullivan

SS/me
Enclosure

HOW THE CALLBACK INTERVIEW DIFFERS FROM THE SCREENING INTERVIEW

Generally speaking, the two interviews differ in the depth of the interviewer's interest. You initiated the first level of interest when you sent your resume to the firm or corporation. That firm or corporation then acknowledged its interest in you by inviting you for a screening interview. The callback interview is the first level of mutual interest—yours by accepting the invitation to interview, theirs by asking you to return to meet more people.

As the first stage of actual mutuality, it is a critical step in the interview process leading to an offer. Let's briefly examine its characteristics.

The callback interview is generally longer in duration than the screening interview. The callback interview usually lasts anywhere from a couple of hours to a full day, during which time you will usually meet several people. Each meeting may take 45 minutes to an hour. Often, one of the meetings will include lunch. You will have an opportunity to discuss your goals and interests as well as to learn more about the people who work at this law firm or corporation.

Callback interviews provide the best picture within which to evaluate a potential employer. It also gives the present employees an opportunity to meet and evaluate you.

Before any interview, research the firm or corporation so that you are as informed as possible. If you are prepared, you will be more relaxed, which will allow your interview to go smoothly.

6

The Importance of Good References

Job seekers often underestimate the importance of references in the job-search process. We have already directed you not to provide any references by name in your resume or cover letter. Usually, you provide references only after you have interviewed with a law firm or corporation and the organization has expressed serious interest in hiring you. Actually, you should not offer references until you have received what is often referred to as "an offer that is contingent upon good references." That means an interested employer has offered you a job, with the contingency that your references must be satisfactory. You must take the word "contingency" seriously; that is, the employer can withdraw an offer if your reference provider expresses any doubt about your capabilities as an attorney or about your qualities as a person. Therefore, you need to choose your references with care.

FACTORS TO CONSIDER IN CHOOSING A REFERENCE PROVIDER

Generally speaking, one reference will be sufficient, unless you are specifically requested to provide more. As the number of references increases, so does the potential for problems. More is not always better. If your present employer does not know you are looking for a new job, asking someone at your place of employment to provide you with a reference may jeopardize your confidentiality. Again, giving serious thought to the possible reactions of the person you ask will help lessen the discomfort of this process.

You should always ask for and receive permission from your reference provider before you release his or her name to a prospective employer. Your request will give you the opportunity to sense what kind of reference you may receive from this person. If you sense that this reference may be ambivalent, negative, or reluctant, you should err on the side of caution and choose another reference who will give you a positive review.

Based on our experience, we recommend that you not formally resign until you know your offer is firm; that is, your reference was good and accepted by your prospective employer. The contrary possibility must be contemplated as well. If your reference provider relays an unacceptable reference, the employer may withdraw the contingent offer leaving your reference provider with the knowledge that you're in the job market. Therefore, be cautious about whom you choose. Ideally, your reference provider should be someone who will give you a great reference, and equally important, someone who will keep your job search in confidence until you formally give notice.

In rare instances, some prospective employers will accept a reference from a prior employer or an attorney who worked with you closely, but who has since made his or her own job change. This situation may allow you to keep your present employer from learning of your job search.

As a rule, however, prospective employers prefer receiving a reference from a partner that you currently work with (if you are working at a law firm) or a senior attorney in your legal department (if you are working at a corporation).

If you didn't realize the importance of the reference check process, we hope this chapter leaves you with no doubt that the person you choose is extremely important.

WHAT IS A PROSPECTIVE EMPLOYER LOOKING FOR IN A REFERENCE CHECK?

Generally speaking, two areas of discussion—the quality of your work product and your qualities as a person—are covered during the brief reference check conversation, usually lasting no more than 15 minutes. First, the reference checker will inquire about the quality of your work product. He or she will ask questions regarding the level of the responsibility you've handled and whether you have met your deadlines. There may also be questions about your writing and negotiating skills and about your ability and maturity in dealing with clients. If you are at a more senior level, the inquirer may want to evaluate your ability to attract clients.

The second area of inquiry is more subjective. Here, the reference checker is interested in matters of personality, cooperation, team effort, and attitude. Questions regarding whether you take direction well, or whether you can lead a group project may come up.

Keep these areas of inquiry in mind, before you set off to locate a suitable reference provider.

7

Examples and Analyses of Inferior Resumes

Over the years, we have received many poorly formatted and disorganized resumes. We formulated much of the information in this book based on our revisions of many such resumes. Hence, to guide you in creating a concise, yet focused resume, we felt it would be useful to include examples of poorly constructed resumes along with explanations of their deficits.

The following resumes demonstrate common and repeated errors in format, organization, or content. In our experience, resumes with such errors do not receive the attention they might otherwise deserve. If you carefully review the examples and our analyses you will be able to avoid these common mistakes when you draft your next resume.

Natalie Burnabee
7889 Crescent Court
Santa Monica, CA 90403
(310)   708-7567

JOB OBJECTIVE: Attorney with a challenging and responsible law firm specializing in appellate law.

SUMMARY OF QUALIFICATIONS:

Over six years' experience analyzing cases, researching, and drafting briefs, motions, legal memos, and pleadings; preparing discovery. Outstanding writing and communication abilities. Adept in leadership and team-player roles.

WHY I AM WELL-QUALIFIED:

Personal strengths, as measured by career expert, Dr. Lynne Presley, include: superior capabilities...enterprising... competitive...goal-oriented...ethical...takes initiative... solves problems independently...resourceful...self-directed...works constructively using good judgment... self-reliant worker...persuasive.

WORK EXPERIENCE: Independent contractor for various attorneys and law firms from 1981 to present.

RESEARCH: Research extensively in the areas of civil litigation, criminal law, and personal injury law.

LEGAL WRITING: Drafted legal memos, appellate briefs, motions, and pleadings. Prepared discovery.

EDUCATION: **Southwestern University**
Los Angeles, California
J.D. 1981

California State University, Long Beach
Long Beach, California
B.A., History, 1977
G.P.A.: 4.0/4.0

HONORS AND CREDITS:

Southwestern Law Review Senior Staff Member, Judicial Externship at the Superior Court with Hon. James Smith. Drafted memos to the Judge re: law and motion cases. Phi Beta Kappa; Dean's List 1975 and 1976.

BAR ADMISSION: State Bar of California, 1981.

Resume 1—Analysis

1. The Job Objective statement is the most overused and ineffective way to communicate the position you are seeking. Try to include this information in your cover letter.

2. The Summary of Qualifications is not necessary if the resume is organized as we have suggested.

3. The Work Experience information should be briefly included within the Employment History paragraph or the Professional Experience paragraph. Furthermore, this description of work experience conveys nothing about specific legal experience.

4. The Research information should be briefly stated within the Employment History paragraph or the Professional Experience paragraph.

5. The Legal Writing information should appear within the Employment History paragraph or the Professional Experience paragraph.

6. The Education paragraph lacks significant information. The complete name of the law school is Southwestern University School of Law, and in addition, no class rank or standing is provided. While it is not mandatory to provide the rank or standing, omitting it implies that your grades are unimpressive and therefore you have chosen not to include them. Omitting class standing information may not inure to your benefit, even if your class standing is not exemplary. The reader may assume a myriad of scenarios about why you have withheld the information, making it unlikely that you will garner an invitation to interview with the potential employer anyway. Consider the consequences of including it or omitting your class rank before you prepare your Education paragraph.

7. The information in the honors and credits section should appear within its appropriate section. The Senior Staff Member position on the *Southwestern Law Review* should appear as an honor with the Southwestern University School of Law information in the Education paragraph; the Phi Beta Kappa and Dean's List honors should be included with the California State University, Long Beach, information in the Education paragraph; and the Externship with the Superior Court belongs in the Employment History paragraph.

CARL STUTTHOFFER
897 Porth Street
Boston, Massachusetts

QUALIFICATIONS

15 years of Senior Corporate Legal Officer experience encompassing:

Legal

* Litigation Management
* Legal Staff Management
* Legislative Analysis/Compliance
* "Preventive Law" Strategies
* ERISA Compliance
* Department Legal Training
* Contract Negotiation/Drafting
* Senior Management Advisor
* Multistate Legal Tracking
* Innovative Legal Strategies
* Acquisitions

* Strategic Planning
* Employee Benefit and Incentive Plans
* Holding Company Strategies
* Securities Compliance
* Marketing Counsel
* Broad Corporate Experience
* Industry Association Effectiveness
* General Corporate and Insurance Tax Issues
* Strong Management Team Member
* Corporate Reorganizations
* Public/Governmental Relations

THE COLONIAL GROUP, INC., Boston, Massachusetts (1987-Present)

General Counsel - Responsible for the Law, Compliance, and New Product departments and all legal matters of this public, insurance/marketing company holding system comprising of 45+ corporations, impacting 1,500 employees and 37,000 agents. Reorganized department responsibilities, internalized certain functions for significant savings and required rendering of timely, practical advice. Important acquisitions were completed and high volume of new products timely implemented. Effective management of high litigation volume.

NEW MEXICO BLUE CROSS & BLUE SHIELD, INC. Albuquerque, New Mexico (1985-1987)

Senior Vice President - Responsible for all Human Resource related functions for 923 stores and 23,000 employees. Reporting areas included six divisional Human Resource departments, Customer Service, Management Services and Corporate Training departments. Participated in corporate strategic planning and decision making as member of Senior Executive Committee. Redesigned, implemented, and administered Employee Benefit/Savings Plans.

EMPLOYER'S REINSURANCE CORPORATION, Overland Park, Kansas (1978-1985)

General Counsel - Senior Vice President, Administration - Responsible for law department, all legal matters affecting the Corporation, and legal counsel to Senior Management, all corporate departments, and 18,000 agents throughout the United States. Also responsible for the management and results of certain administrative departments. Effectively coordinated with legal counterparts in two levels of upstream companies and multitude of related corporations. Close legal advisor to all senior officers. Molded law department and staff into important and successful contributor to corporate effort. Implemented law department PC network, electronic research capability, and database retention.

FEDERATED MUTUAL INSURANCE COMPANY, Owatonna, Minnesota (1971-1978)

Legal Counsel - Legal counsel to large and diverse number of departments and effectively managed outside counsel and large number of litigations. Heavily involved in legislative and governmental issues.

SIGNIFICANT ACCOMPLISHMENTS

*   Conducted search, due diligence, and negotiation of important acquisition. Created related corporations and negotiated contract establishing national network. Will save $3 million the first year and $10 million in later years. Negotiated and concluded other acquisitions.

*   Heavy participation in national associations and state insurance federation.

*   Negotiated new employee insurance and benefit package resulting in $4 million savings and established new service standards for carrier. Also redesigned and installed new Employee Savings and Profit Sharing Plans.

*   Solid expertise in contract negotiation, drafting, and interpretation.

*   Experienced and effective in state and federal government relations.

*   Led effort to create corporated procedures responsive to AIDS prior to most companies.

*   Negotiated substantial office lease package yielding $1.8 million in cash concession and extremely favorable rate and renewal options.

*   Major contributor in the development and implementation of national sales campaign which affected the standards and philosphy of the life insurance industry.

*   Instituted "preventative law" program that reduced outstanding litigations by 60%.

*   Formulated and executed agent-owned reinsurance company concept.

*   Consistent practitioner of team building, communication, and leadership.

*   Effective participant in senior executive strategies and decision making.

*   Consistently enhanced credibility and professionalism of law departments by establishing clear attorney-department responsibilities.

PROFESSIONAL AFFILIATIONS

County, State, and U.S. Bar Association Member, Chartered Life Underwriter, Chartered Financial Consultant, American Life Insurance Counsel Association Member

EDUCATION

J.D., John Marshall Law School, Chicago, Illinois,1971
B.A., Business Administration, Methodist College, Fayetteville, North Carolina, 1967

Resume 2—Analysis

1. The name, address, and phone number information at the top of the resume should be complete, including zip code and home phone number.

2. The Qualifications section is not necessary if the resume is organized as we have suggested.

3. The 22 items of legal experience preceded by an asterisk should be drafted in prose-style within a Professional Experience paragraph. The use of lists and asterisks (or bullets) is distracting and unprofessional. Furthermore, merely listing the legal experience does not give the reader a sense of the depth of the experience.

4. The work experience information should be organized with the dates of employment in the left margin and the name, city, and state of the employer indented beneath the date. Since the employment experience is varied, the experience can be listed separately under the appropriate employer.

5. The Significant Accomplishments section unnecessarily uses a second page. Furthermore, the 13 entries preceded by an asterisk should be included within the Professional Experience paragraph or within the context of specific duties and/or responsibilities under each employment entry in the Employment History paragraph.

6. The Professional Affiliations paragraph lists "Chartered Life Underwriter," "Chartered Financial Consultant," and "American Life Insurance Counsel Association Member," which are not legal professional affiliations. Again, consider carefully whether the information you include enhances your resume.

7. The Education paragraph fails to include significant information. No class rank or standing is provided for John Marshall Law School, and no grade-point average is provided for Methodist College. While it is not mandatory to provide the rank, standing, or grade-point average, omitting it implies that your grades are unimpressive and therefore you have chosen not to include them. Omitting class standing or grade-point average information may not inure to your benefit, even if your class standing or grade-point average is not exemplary. The reader may assume a myriad of scenarios about why you have withheld the information, making it unlikely that you will garner an invitation to interview with the potential employer anyway. Consider the consequences of including or omitting your class rank before you prepare your Education paragraph.

THOMAS R. ANGELOPOLOUS
8976 Vineyard Road
Dallas, Texas 75206
(214)978-6789

OBJECTIVE:

A position as corporate counsel or equivalent level business position, which will utilize my *legal, business,* and *international* education and experience. I am currently earning $72,000 per year and am seeking an annual salary of $82,000.

PROFILE:

Extensive legal knowledge in all aspects of corporate practice**Thrive on challenging projects**Equally effective working independently or collaboratively**Superior writing, drafting and editing skills**Bilingual (English/Spanish)

EDUCATION:

Juris Doctor, American University College of Law, 1991

Bachelor of Arts, History and English, Vanderbilt University, 1988

* *Course work included financial and management accounting, comparative economics and commercial Spanish*

PROFESSIONAL EXPERIENCE:

Associate Attorney, Jackson & Walker, Dallas, Texas   1991-Present

Experience in a broad range of legal areas, including mergers and acquisitions, corporations, partnerships, litigation, securities, employment matters, immigration, real estate and bankruptcy.

* Assisted in acquisition of U.S. assets of a Spanish manufacturing company, including real estate and facilities in Delaware, Florida, and Pennsylvania. Drafted transfer documents for patents pending and tax permits and research and obtained all regulatory approvals.

* Prepared necessary research and documentation and interfaced with Federal and State regulatory agencies regarding the $4 million purchase of a stockyard and livestock auction facility in Oklahoma.

* Experienced in formation of corporations, partnerships, and complex ownership structures, including tax, shareholder, employment, and licensing issues.

* Performed all work required to qualify an insurance agency in all 50 states.

* Researched and implemented defensive strategies for a defendant corporation, including amending shareholder buy-sell agreement, officer employment agreements, and license agreements.

* Drafted brief for computer copyright litigation.

* Knowledgeable in employer/employee matters such as covenants not to compete and independent contractor agreements.

* Finalized settlement of suit between a domestic corporation and a Canadian landlord.

* Redrafted group health insurance policies, requiring approval of State Insurance Commissioners.

ADDITIONAL EXPERIENCE AND QUALIFICATIONS:

* Attended William and Mary School of Law Program in Madrid, Spain, in 1990.

* Wrote and published articles on international topics.

* Coached and judged moot court arguments.

* Served an internship at the Washington Legal Foundation, Washington, DC, 1988.

AFFILIATIONS:

American Bar Association
State Bar of Texas
Dallas Bar Association

Resume 3—Analysis

1. The job objective statement is the most overused and ineffective way to communicate the position you are seeking. Furthermore, a resume should never include an individual's present compensation and/or compensation requirements.

2. The Profile section is not necessary if the resume is organized as we have suggested. This information should be included within the Professional Experience paragraph. Language capabilities should be listed under a separate heading.

3. The Education paragraph fails to include significant information. The complete name of the law school is American University Washington College of Law. In addition, no class rank or standing is provided for American University and no grade-point average is provided for Vanderbilt University. While it is not mandatory to provide the class rank, standing, or grade-point average, omitting it implies that your grades are unimpressive and therefore you have chosen not to include them. Even if your class standing or grade-point average is not exemplary, omitting class standing or grade-point average information may not inure to your benefit. If the reader assumes a myriad of scenarios about why you have withheld the information, you are unlikely to garner an invitation to interview with the potential employer anyway. Consider the consequences of including or omitting your class rank before you prepare your Education paragraph.

4. The Professional Experience paragraph includes only one legal employment position. Hence, that information can appear under a single employment entry. However, the section heading should be "Employment," and the dates of employment should appear in the left margin. The position held, "Associate," should appear below the name, city, and state of the law firm. In addition, the experience should not be set up as a list with asterisks (or bullets) and double spaces separating the items. Instead it should appear in one prose-style paragraph. Again, try to conserve space so that your resume appears on one page. Since this attorney graduated in 1991 and has had only one legal job, his resume should fit comfortably on one page.

5. The Additional Experience and Qualifications paragraph is unnecessary; the information can be included in the appropriate sections. The William and Mary Program in Madrid should be listed under the Law School entry in the Education paragraph. Unless "Coaching and judging moot court arguments" is an honor, it should not be included. If it is an honor, it should be listed as an

honor under the Law School entry. The internship at the Washington Legal Foundation should be briefly included in the Employment History paragraph.

6. The Affiliations paragraph fails to include the date of admission. The omission of the date implies that you may not have passed the bar on the first attempt. Even if you did not pass the bar on the first attempt, you should nevertheless include the date of admission to the State Bar.

DONALD Q. ROBINSON
3489 Cranberry Lane
Chicago, Illinois 60611
(302)   786-3647

EDUCATION

Legal

1989	U.C.L.A.	JD		Law
		LSAT score 44 (top 4%)		GPA: 80.311 (top 22%)

Graduate

1982	U.C.L.A.	MA	History

Undergraduate

1980	U.S.C.	BA	History (major)

AWARDS AND ORGANIZATION MEMBERSHIP

Member   Illinois Bar
Phi Beta Kappa   Undergraduate Honorary

EMPLOYMENT EXPERIENCE

1989 - Present   THIRD-YEAR ASSOCIATE/ LAW CLERK
Summer 1988   Sidley & Austin
                        One First National Plaza
                        Chicago, Illinois

1982-1986   PROFESSOR OF HISTORY
                        U.C.L.A.
                        Los Angeles, California

LEGAL TRAINING

First Year: Contracts, Criminal Law I, Criminal Law II, Civil Procedure, Property, Legal Research & Writing, Torts.
Second Year: Antitrust, Labor Law, Evidence, Business Associations, Constitutional Law I & II, Corporate Finance, Federal Taxation I.
Third Year: Chattel Security & Commercial Property, Environmental Law, Remedies, Trial Advocacy, Wills & Trusts, Community Property.

Experience with on-line legal research: Lexis, Westlaw.

LEGAL EXPERIENCE

Corporate and Business Law:
Helped draft opinion letter for a business acquisition.
Researched potential newspaper advertising liabilities.
Drafted a partnership dissolution agreement.
Drafted letters to clients.

LEGAL EXPERIENCE (CONT'D)

Prepared closing documents for an asset securitization transaction and negotiated certain governing law provisions with opposing counsel.

Research franchise investment law on potential liabilities regarding dealership termination.

Dealt directly with clients over the phone.

Researched cold storage warehouse law and licensing requirements.

Researched anti-competition clauses.

Researched suretyship issues.

Compared the bylaws of a consumer cooperative corporation with requirements under Illinois Corporations law.

Researched mechanic's liens law on protective devices for the lender with respect to a multimillion dollar loan.

Attended several bankruptcy hearings on behalf of a creditor.

Real Estate Law:

Helped to prepare all closing documents for a lease purchase.

Drafted purchase agreements for sale of properties.

Drafted opinion letter request to be sent to Department of Real Estate regarding a broker's license.

Researched Subdivision Map Act.

Researched lease holdover liabilities.

Drafted legal memorandum to be distributed to S & A clients regarding real estate appraisal requirements under the federal law, Financial Institutions Reform, Recovery, and Enforcement Act of 1989 ("FIRREA").

Tax Law:

Helped write small portion of an outline on tax aspects of Japanese investments in United States real estate.

Investigated status of proposed tax bill through contact with legislative aides.

Researched feasibility of corporate reorganization into subchaper S.

Researched issue of when a sale takes place for federal income tax purposes.

Researched criminal sanctions for violation of federal tax law (to advise client regarding a pending deposition).

Securities Law:

Researched Section 16 changes and Rule 144 restrictions on the sale of securities.

Conducted on - site due diligence for a securities offering.

Banking and Finance:

Prepared a closing checklist for a bank loan transaction.

Pro Bono Corporate:

Incorporation of a public benefit corporation and application for tax exempt status.

Litigation:

Drafted motion to compel arbitration and to stay proceedings.

Drafted defendant's motion for summary judgment.

Researched labor law actions and the statute of limitations.

Resume 4—Analysis

1. The Education paragraph has an unusual format. The spacing, indenting, and column style makes this paragraph difficult to read. This example demonstrates how the format can distract the reader's attention from focusing on a well-credentialed attorney's educational qualifications. Here, form takes on more focus than content. Even though U.C.L.A. and U.S.C. are often referred to by their acronyms, all universities and colleges should be spelled out in their full form: U.C.L.A. should read: University of California, at Los Angeles and U.S.C. should read: University of Southern California.

2. The Awards and Organization Membership paragraph is unnecessary. The information here should appear in the appropriate sections. For example, the Illinois Bar Membership should appear under its own heading, "Bar Admission," and should include the date of admission. In addition, the Phi Beta Kappa designation should appear in the Education paragraph under the undergraduate entry of University of Southern California.

3. The Employment Experience paragraph is formatted incorrectly. The dates of employment should be flush to the left margin. The employment position entry should state the employer on the first line, the city and state on the second line, and the position held on the third line. It is not necessary to indicate the "Class Year Associate" level attained. The reader will be able to discern from the year of law school graduation what the Class Year level is. If there is a Class Year discrepancy (e.g., you are a fourth-year associate, but for purposes of salary you are treated as a third-year associate), you do not need to include that in your resume; however, you may choose to mention it in your cover letter. In addition, the Sidley & Austin entry should not include the street address.

4. The Legal Training paragraph is unnecessary. Most legal employers have attended law school and are aware of law school course study. Including this information adds nothing to the attorney's marketability and is a poor use of space. Furthermore, if the attorney has submitted a transcript with his resume, the law school course study will be itemized. In addition, it is unnecessary to specify experience in Lexis and/or Westlaw, because it does not appreciably enhance the applicant's abilities as an attorney.

5. The Legal Experience paragraphs consume more than one page and include experience in seven areas of practice. Let's examine this "Legal Experience" section carefully. First, we can assume that all the experience was obtained as Sidley & Austin, the only legal

employer that appears on this resume. Second, it demonstrates that, as a junior associate, the attorney rotated through several departments within the law firm and received myriad assignments from different departments. Therefore, it indicates that the attorney has yet to specialize in one area of practice. Third, the pertinent and appropriate legal experience information should appear within the Professional Experience paragraph or be included under the Employment History entry of Sidley & Austin.

6. Keep in mind that the resume is a marketing tool. If drafted and used properly, the resume can open doors of opportunity for you. Hence, if this attorney is applying to a potential employer who has a need for a real estate attorney, he should consider carefully the purpose of including areas of practice that do not relate to real estate. Some might say, "Well, it doesn't hurt to include it." However, an argument can be made that it does hurt. If the attorney has experience in all these other areas of practice, the employer may query how much actual experience he possesses in real estate. The inclusion of the other areas of practice diverts the focus from the experience in real estate toward the other six areas of practice. Furthermore, the additional information is not related to the position being sought and pushes the resume onto an unnecessary second page.

PAUL ARBARGINO
173 Via Veneto
Rome, Italy
(011-67-89)

PROFESSIONAL EXPERIENCE

**January 1989 -
Present**   **BAKER & McKENZIE**
Commercial Department, **Rome office** (January 1991 - present). I
maintain a general corporate practice including mergers and acquisitions
and joint ventures as well as advising on environmental issues arising
on commercial transactions. I continue to develop relations with finance
and banking clients. I was primarily responsible for obtaining bondholder
approval in difficult circumstances (involved detailed negotiations and
settlement with secured lenders) for the disposal of a well-known leasing
business for approximately $3 billion.

Transferred to the Commercial Department of Baker & Mckenzie, **San
Francisco, California office** (July 1989 -December 1990). I
was involved in drafting and negotiating mergers and acquisitions, joint
ventures, corporate reorganizations, licensing, franchise, distribution
and employment agreements, and credit facilities. I advised on a wide range
of general corporate matters including establishing local and
offshore corporations, shareholder rights and director's liabilities,
bankruptcy and insolvency, tax, immigration, and statutory and
contractual requirements. Also, I advised local and international banking
clients on a range of issues including licensing requirements, obtaining
guarantees from offshore corporations, lender liability issues, and
software licenses. In addition, I gained expertise in issues relating to
electronic funds transfer (EFT), including on transactional basis assisting
with the merger of EFT networks in southeastern United States.

Commercial Department, **Rome office** (January 1989 - June 1989).
I advised on, prepared, and negotiated finance and banking matters of a
substantial and complex nature (including credit facilities and collateral,
offshore investment funds, bond issues, and regulatory concerns).
Primary person in Rome responsible for advising on regulatory issues
relating to financial services and insurance, including advising on
obtaining relevant authorizations and applicable compliance requirements.
Also responsible for and coordinated substantial and complex general
corporate transactions, including mergers and acquisitions, joint
ventures, corporate reorganizations as well as advising generally on
contractual, tax, competition, and labor issues. (I was, for example, in
charge of and responsible for the disposal of a group of hotels in Italy for
approximately $8 billion).

PERSONAL

Born in Rome, Italy, September 25, 1960.
Married.
Citizenship - Italy and United States.

EDUCATION

Rome University, Rome
Law Degree, 1989 Upper Third

SPECIAL INTERESTS AND SKILLS

I enjoy theater, tennis, horseback riding, and squash. I have traveled extensively in the United States, Europe, and Japan. Enjoy collecting antiques, particularly Japanese furniture and Turkish kilims.

Resume 5—Analysis

1. The name, address, and home phone number should be centered at the top of the resume. Even though this applicant lives and works in Rome, he should provide a contact address and phone number in the United States.

2. The Professional Experience section could be renamed "Employment," since it includes employment information. In addition, the description of experience should never be written in the first person. Instead of "I maintain a general corporate practice . . . ," the resume should state, "General corporate practice includes mergers and acquisitions . . ."

3. The Personal paragraph should not include birth or marriage information. While citizenship information is not usually included, it may be wise to indicate it, if you feel you may be questioned about a Work Permit Visa.

4. The Education paragraph fails to include significant information. There is no entry for an undergraduate college or university. Furthermore, the law school entry of Rome University in Rome should appear in four lines, as follows:

Rome University
Rome, Italy
Law Degree, 1989
Class Standing: Upper Third.

5. The Special Interests and Skills paragraph should be renamed "Personal Interests." In addition, the information should not be written in the first person. For example, "I enjoy theater," should simply read, "Theater and tennis."

6. This resume, with the modifications we have suggested, should fit on one page.

DOROTHY WASSERSTEIN
673 Hazelwood Drive, Apt. 1233
New York, New York 10022
(212)   765-3490

OBJECTIVE

To obtain an insurance defense litigation associate position.

BAR MEMBERSHIP

New York, 1991

EXPERIENCE

ASSOCIATE
Herzfeld & Rubin
New York, New York
October 1991 to Present
Handle insurance defense cases, including reports of liability, discovery, and motions.

SUMMER ASSOCIATE
Issler & Schrage
New York, New York
May 1990 to August 1990
Researched and drafted motions and memoranda in the areas of insurance defense, municipal liability, and law enforcement. Assisted in discovery and trial preparation.

BODILY INJURY CLAIM ADJUSTER
Atlantic Mutual Insurance Company
New York, New York
November 1986 to August 1988
Investigated, negotiated, and settled claims.

EDUCATION

CARDOZA SCHOOL OF LAW
New York, New York
J.D. May 1991
Class Rank: Top 20%
Associate Editor, Law Review

STATE UNIVERSITY OF NEW YORK, STONY BROOK
Stony Brook, New York
B.A. 1986, English, *cum laude*

PERSONAL

Traveling, sailing, and garage sales.

REFERENCES

Samuel I. Cohen, Esq.
Issler & Schrage
New York, New York
(212)   768-2200

Peter Carroway
Atlantic Mutual Ins. Co.
New York, New York
(212)   788-9900

Resume 6—Analysis

1. A Job Objective statement is the most overused and ineffective way to communicate the position you are seeking. Try to include this information in your cover letter.

2. The Bar Membership paragraph is an important part of the resume. However, it should appear at the end of this resume. A potential employer's first interest is in knowing your Education and Experience background, then in learning when and where you were admitted to practice.

3. The Experience section is formatted incorrectly and should be renamed "Employment." First, the dates of employment should appear flush to the left margin. Second, the position held, "Associate" or "Summer Associate," should appear in the third line of information; the law firm, rather than the position, should be emphasized and typed in bold. Third, the associate and summer associate positions involved the same area of practice. Hence, this attorney should draft a Professional Experience paragraph that includes the work experience separately. Where you have practiced within the same area of expertise for more than one year and with more than one employer, the Professional Experience paragraph aids in streamlining your resume. We have generally advised not to include nonlegal experience. However, this applicant has worked in the area of insurance, which may enhance her ability to practice insurance defense. Therefore, it may be useful to include this experience in the Employment paragraph. The position held should be the third sentence. The sentence explaining her experience at Atlantic Mutual Insurance Company is brief enough to keep within the employment entry.

4. The Education paragraph is formatted properly; however, a few items require mention. Under the law school entry, the proper name is Yeshiva University, Benjamin N. Cardozo School of Law. The J.D. award need not include the month (May); the year (1991) is sufficient. Unless you graduate at an unusual time of year, the month of graduation is irrelevant. The words *Class Rank* should be underlined. The complete name of the journal, *Cardozo Law Review,* should be stated and underlined. The undergraduate entry is complete, except that the order of the items in the third line should read: B.A. *cum laude,* English, 1986.

5. The Personal paragraph includes three items. Traveling and sailing are appropriate interests and may encourage your interviewer to engage in a conversation. However, a potential employer may consider "garage sales" inappropriate or unprofessional. Furthermore,

and more importantly, this subject is unlikely to encourage conversation. Remember, the purpose of this section is to try to evoke common interests.

6. We have discussed in detail why the inclusion of references is inappropriate. Even though the references in this example are prior employers and do not breach confidentiality at your present employment, responding to any potential employer's inquiries may, nevertheless, place undue burden on your reference providers. It is better that they be contacted when a potential employer has expressed serious interest in hiring you. State that you will provide references by including the sentence "References Available Upon Request" at the bottom of your resume.

MELVIN KLINGER
7896 Liberty Ave, Apt. No. 185
Philadelphia, Pennsylvania
(215)   956-4565

SUMMARY

Senior Counsel experienced in successful legal support to large and small companies in High Tech/Data Processing, Finance, Communications, and Health Care industries. Track record as Vice President, Secretary and Chief Legal Counsel, achieving significant reductions in risk and securing advantageous business terms. Developed successful relationships with vendors and customers.

KEY AREAS OF EXPERTISE

Intellectual property transactions, procurement of telecommunication services, litigation management, protection of proprietary rights, acquisitions, and joint ventures.

REPRESENTATIVE ACCOMPLISHMENTS

*   Drafted scores of software development agreements. One for image processing check system will generate savings of over $100 million.

*   Established consortium of companies to seek FCC license to provide mobile communication services. Initial funding of partnership was $40 million. Projected annual revenues over $300 million.

*   Disposed of unprofitable product lines. Generated cash and royalty payments of several million dollars.

*   Sold data processing services to Beachead University Hospital and others. Total revenue in excess of $60 million.

*   Negotiated, reviewed, and drafted significant numbers of software licenses and software distribution agreements.

*   Established proprietary rights program to protect software developments.

*   Successfully secured consents to transfers to software license agreements and rejected vendor claims in excess of $4 million as part of bank merger.

*   Negotiated Tariff 12 Custom Telephone Service Agreements. Savings over $12 million.

*   Acquisition of numerous health care facilities. Largest transaction involved was aborted purchase of Crescent Moon Hospital for $300 million.

EMPLOYMENT

CORESTATES FINANCIAL CORPORATION and   Jan. 1988 - Present
THE PHILADELPHIA NATIONAL BANK
Vice President and Associate Counsel

Provide legal services to Corestates Financial Corporation. Companywide responsibility for trademarks, patents, and copyrights.

BELL ATLANTIC CORPORATION   Feb. 1987 - Dec. 1987
Vice President and Senior Corporate Counsel

Provided legal support related to buyouts, financings, FCC licensing, and international and domestic joint ventures.

PHILADELPHIA NEWSPAPERS, INC.   Jan. 1986 - Jan. 1987
Chief Legal Counsel and Secretary

Responsible for the general legal affairs. Services related to FCC licensing, international and domestic joint ventures, and acquisitions.

WYETH LABORATORIES   Feb. 1978 - Dec. 1985
Law Clerk, Assistant General Counsel, Corporate Counsel

Provided antitrust and general advice in connection with the sale and marketing of pharmaceuticals. Assured FDA compliance and reviewed all marketing plans and activities for compliance with antitrust consent decree.

EDUCATION

Juris Doctor, University of Pennsylvania (Class Rank: Top 15%), 1978

Bachelor of Arts, Stanford University (Class Rank: Top 3%), 1975

MEMBERSHIPS

State Bar of Pennsylvania, 1978

American Bar Association - Patent, Trademark and Copyright Law Section

State Bar of Pennsylvania - Intellectual Property Section

Philadelphia County Bar Association

Resume 7—Analysis

1. The Summary paragraph is not necessary if the resume is organized as we have suggested.

2. The Key Areas of Expertise section is unnecessary. Instead, this information should be included in a professional Experience paragraph highlighting this attorney's legal experience.

3. The Representative Accomplishments section in this sample resume is discretionary. Although the experience could be presented within the Professional Experience paragraph or the Employment History paragraph, the present format is acceptable for highlighting the extensive experience of this senior attorney (Class Year 1978). In this example, the names of two clients, Beachead University Hospital and Crescent Moon Hospital are specified. Never reveal the name of and the work performed for a client. Furthermore, do not use asterisks (or bullets) to highlight information. This style is distracting and unprofessional. These accomplishments should not appear on the first page; either create an addendum to your resume or place the section on a second page. A potential employer reviewing the first page of this resume would first read the least important information. Never place your most impressive information on the second page. A reader who is unimpressed with your first page may not read further on.

4. The Employment section is formatted incorrectly. First, the dates should appear flush to the left margin. Second, this attorney has had four jobs. Each position is briefly described and only states "provided legal services" or "provided advice." Since this is not significant information, the Professional Experience paragraph should be utilized and should include the items from the Representative Accomplishments section.

5. The Education paragraph fails to include essential information. The city and state is absent from the University of Pennsylvania and from Stanford University. The undergraduate major is absent from the Stanford University entry. Also, stylistically, the words "Class Rank" should be underlined. The most glaring error of the format of this resume, however, is that the strongest aspects of this resume appear on the second page. The academic achievements of this attorney are impressive and yet they appear as two lines of information near the bottom of the second page. As we have reiterated, strategize your strongest assets by placing them boldly and prominently within your resume. Do not bury them on a second page. In this example, the Education paragraph should have appeared on the first page after the Professional Experience paragraph.

6. The Memberships section is acceptable; however, the author could minimize space by including the items in a continuous line separated by semicolons:

State Bar of Pennsylvania, 1978; State Bar of Pennsylvania (Intellectual Property Section); American Bar Association (Patent, Trademark, and Copyright Law Section); Philadelphia County Bar Association.

In the sample resume, these items take up four lines, each separated by a double space. Ironically, the attorney allocated more space and attention to the Membership section than to his Education paragraph. Again, ask yourself whether a potential employer would be more impressed and interested in your bar memberships and activities or your academic achievements. Remember to analyze the space allocation of your resume in terms of its marketing yourself as a potential new hire.

PATRICK O'SHANAHAN

SPECIALIZATION:	Employee Benefits, Executive Compensation, Employment Taxes and Exempt Organizations
EDUCATION:	LL.M. (Taxation), New York University (1985) J.D., Yale Law School (1984) M.A., Carnegie-Mellon University (1979) B.A., University of Pittsburgh (1977)
ADMITTED:	New York

Patrick O'Shanahan joined Shearman & Sterling as an associate in 1988. Prior to joining Shearman & Sterling, Mr. O'Shanahan was an attorney with the Bachelder Law Firm in New York. There his practice focused on employee benefits, executive compensation and exempt organizations. As a law clerk, Mr. O'Shanahan worked with Kaye, Scholer, Fierman, Hays & Handler, in their New York office, where he handled employee benefit, executive, and international tax matters.

Mr. O'Shanahan is an author of several chapters in the Matthew Bender Federal Tax Service on tax qualified deferred compensation plans (1991). He has also published articles on a variety of subjects in the Yale Law Journal (1989).

Mr. O'Shanahan is a continuing bar education instuctor in New York. Mr. O'Shanahan has made numerous presentations to professional and business organizations.

Mr. O'Shanahan has several references that are prepared to speak at length about his professional legal career, as well as his personal attributes.

Resume 8—Analysis

1. This resume does not include an address and home phone number. Without this vital information, the attorney leaves the reader with only one way to contact him; namely, at his present employer Shearman & Sterling. This scenario poses the problem that the present employer may learn that Mr. O'Shanahan is looking for a new job.

2. The Specialization section is unnecessary if the resume is organized as we have suggested. This information should be included in the Professional Experience paragraph rather than the Education paragraph, because the attorney has practiced in the same expertise for more than one year and with more than one employer.

3. The Education paragraph fails to include significant information. For example, the city and state is absent from all four educational institutions. In addition, there is no indication of class rank, class standing, or grade-point average information. The undergraduate major is absent from the University of Pittsburgh entry. The graduate degree obtained at Carnegie-Mellon University does not indicate in what major it was obtained.

4. The Admitted section does not include the date of admission to the bar.

5. The next four prose paragraphs each deal with a significant aspect of Mr. O'Shanahan's career; namely, employment, publications, teaching, and references. Each has its place within the resume. However, the present format is unacceptable and unprofessional and does not convey the information in a manner that is likely to garner the attention of a potential employer. Equally important is that the resume should not be in the third person. Let's review each paragraph:

1. The first paragraph discusses the employment of the attorney. It concisely states Mr. O'Shanahan's three places of legal employment; however, it does not include the dates of employment. Instead of narrative prose, the three employment situations should use the format previously described.

2. The second paragraph discusses the publications written by the attorney. It briefly states that Mr. O'Shanahan is an author of several articles, however, it does not specifically name the articles. The information should be included in a section headed "Publications" with the specifics of each article, date, and place of publication.

3. The third paragraph explains that the attorney is an instructor with the continuing bar education in New York and has made presentations to organizations. This information should be included in the section headed Bar Admissions and Activities. The courses taught should be indicated along with the dates. The names of the professional presentations should be named along with the dates.

4. The fourth paragraph briefly states that the attorney has references. Again, this fact is simply expressed by the following sentence, "References Available Upon Request."

ROBERT A. MARTINEZ
567 Agua Fria, Apt. No. 2
Santa Fe, New Mexico 87501
(505)   458-8721

EDUCATION

J.D., University of Notre Dame, Notre Dame, Indiana, 1991
*Top 10%
*Participant, Trial Advocacy Program
*American Jurisprudence Award: Appellate Advocacy

B.A., Political Science, University of New Mexico, Albuquerque, New Mexico, 1988
*G.P.A.: 3.8/4.0

LEGAL EXPERIENCE

1991 to Present   ASSOCIATE, Montgomery & Andrews, Santa Fe, New Mexico
                  *Depositions   *Trial & Appellate Practice
                  *Hearings   *Complex Oil & Gas Litigation

1990 to 1991   LAW CLERK, May, Oberfell & Lorber, South Bend, Indiana
                  * Products Liability Litigation

                  EXTERN, Honorable Carey Mapeworth, Judge, U.S. District Court for
                  Southern District of Indiana

OTHER WORK EXPERIENCE

Summer 1987   Oshman's Sporting Goods
                  Villa Linda Mall
                  Santa Fe, New Mexico
                  Fly Fishing Sales Representative

Summer 1986   New Wave Rafting Company
                  Santa Fe, New Mexico
                  River Rafting Guide

PUBLICATION

Fly Fishing on the Banks of the Colorado River, American Sportsman,
(September 1992).

HOBBIES AND INTERESTS

Writing, fly fishing, and skiing.

Resume 9—Analysis

1. The Education paragraph has an unusual format. The use of indented information and asterisks (or bullets) distracts the reader. In addition, since the attorney graduated several years ago, his participation in the University of Notre Dame's Trial Advocacy Program is attenuated in value. Unless it is an honor, it should not be included. The American Jurisprudence Award in Appellate Advocacy should be listed as an honor, with the word "honor" underlined.

2. The Legal Experience section is not formatted properly. The employment position entry should state the employer on the first line and the position held on the third line. In addition, the positions held need not be in capital letters. Capitalizing words brings attention to them. Analyze carefully what you want to emphasize. Asterisks are distracting, and the information does not detail the responsibilities at each law firm. The litigation practice and experience should be detailed either in a Professional Experience paragraph or under each employment position. The description need not be lengthy; however, "one-word lines or phrases" do not provide a potential employer with the depth of your legal experience. The extern position entry neglects to include the dates of employment.

3. The Other Work Experience section information in this example is irrelevant to the legal position Mr. Martinez is applying for. The main objective of your attorney resume is to demonstrate to a potential employer why you are qualified for a position as an attorney. While the experience included is not inherently inappropriate, it does not enhance the resume. The resume is a marketing tool. If drafted and used properly, the resume can open doors of opportunity for you. Hence, consider carefully what to include in your resume as well as what to exclude.

4. The Publication section is an important one and when used appropriately can enhance a resume. However, while Mr. Martinez's published article in the *American Sportsman* is impressive, it does not directly relate to his ability as an attorney. (If the attorney had written an article dealing with the legalities of fishing on the banks of the Colorado River, which then appeared in the *Legislative Journal of Game & Fishing* concerning Code Section 980 (a) 2(b), it would be appropriate to include it.) Again, the attorney resume should highlight your ability as an attorney.

5. The Hobbies and Interests paragraph is acceptable; however, the heading "Personal Interests" is succinct and includes all possible and appropriate interests.

PAULA CARSON ROLLINS
344 Sunshine Court
Miami, Florida 33133
(305) 441-8990

EDUCATION

TULANE UNIVERSITY OF LOUISIANA, New Orleans, Louisiana
Juris Doctor, 1986
Graduated *cum laude*
Tulane Law Review, Member

UNIVERSITY OF FLORIDA, Gainesville, Florida
Bachelor of Arts, English, 1983
G.P.A.: 4.0/4.0

LEGAL EXPERIENCE

Nov. 1986 to Present   **STROOCK & STROOCK & LAVAN,** Miami, Florida
Associate.
Broad range of transactional experience including secured lending, bankruptcy workouts, legal opinions, public finance, general corporate issues, banking regulation, and securities regulation. Additional experience includes drafting motions briefs, complaints, discovery, and research memoranda.

Summer 1985   **LISKOW & LEWIS,** New Orleans, Louisiana
Summer Associate.
Researched and wrote legal memoranda in the areas of corporate securities, real estate, and litigation. Drafted corporate documents.

CONTINUING EDUCATION
*Counseling Clients in the Entertainment Industry-PLI Seminar
*Entertainment, Art and Sports Law-PLI Seminar
*Organizing and Advising Partnerships and Joint Ventures-CEB Seminar
*Member, American Bar Association's Forum on the Entertainment and Sports Industries, Patent, Trademark, and Copyright Law and Intellectual Property Section

BAR ADMISSION
State Bar of Florida, 1986

PERSONAL
Married seven years to Todd Rollins. Three children, Rachel 6 years old, Robert 4 years old, and Randi 15 months. Enjoy scuba diving, snorkeling, and nude sunbathing. Professional model during college.

Resume 10—Analysis

1. This resume is formatted in a disorganized manner. The lack of margin continuity causes visual distraction. Some information is flush to the left margin, other information appears at various indented positions. Keep your resume uniform, so that the form becomes an invisible vehicle for presenting the information. The content of your resume should draw the reader's attention, not the form.

2. The Education paragraph is formatted correctly; however, a few items require mention. The city and state should appear as the second line under the law school name and undergraduate name. The *cum laude* designation can appear on the third line with the J.D. award: Juris Doctorate, *cum laude,* 1986. The undergraduate entry appears incomplete. First, the acronym G.P.A. should be underlined to draw attention to it. Second, since the attorney graduated from the University of Florida with a 4.0 average, it would seem that she may have graduated *summa cum laude* or *magna cum laude.* If so, this designation should be included.

3. The Experience section is formatted incorrectly and should be renamed "Employment." First, the dates of employment should not be abbreviated. There is enough room in the left margin to spell out the month: November. Second, the city and state of each law firm should appear in the second line. Third, the "Associate" position held at Stroock & Stroock & Lavan since 1986 does not detail the area of practice held. Since no Professional Experience paragraph was used, the Employment History paragraph should be detailed to indicate the specific area of practice. This attorney simply names six independent corporate transactional practice areas and mentions nothing about her exact duties. Also, she includes litigation experience. Again, an associate who has over seven years of legal experience should be able to indicate specific experience. Should the areas of practice overlap, then include each area as we have suggested. Third, since the Summer Associate position at Liskow & Lewis ended eight years ago, it does not require a detailed experience paragraph. Instead, simply state the position held—"Summer Associate"—and whether an offer was extended.

4. Continuing Education is an unnecessary section. First, legal employers presume that you take courses that enhance your legal practice, so it is unnecessary to list them. In this example, there is no direct connection between the Associate's corporate practice at Stroock & Stroock & Lavan in Miami and the predominantly entertainment and sports law continuing education coursework. Because

the material is irrelevant to the attorney's practice of law, it should be excluded, but the attorney may be trying to stretch her entertainment coursework to overcome her lack of direct experience in the area of entertainment law. Usually this attempt makes a potential employer aware that the attorney does not possess direct experience for the position being sought and is attempting to substitute class study. Therefore, do not include such information on a resume. If it adds to your interest in a particular area of practice or may influence a hiring decision, then include it in your cover letter or mention it during your interview. The last entry in this section "Member, American Bar Association" should appear in the Bar Admission paragraph.

5. The Bar Membership paragraph is alright; however, it should include any memberships in the American Bar Association.

6. The Personal paragraph includes marital status, name of spouse, and names and ages of children. As we have discussed, these matters do not directly relate to a person's ability to practice law and therefore should not appear on a resume. The two interests of scuba diving and snorkeling are appropriate personal interests and may encourage an interviewer to engage in a conversation. However, "nude sunbathing" may be considered inappropriate or unprofessional by a potential employer. The statement "Professional model during college" does not enhance the person's abilities as an attorney. It is non-legal employment that has no bearing on legal experience or practice.

LISA CHANG, ESQ.
3980 Prescott Avenue
Seattle, Washington 98101
(206) 787-5431

EDUCATION
Graduate: **HASTINGS COLLEGE OF THE LAW**
San Francisco, California
Awarded Juris Doctorate in May 1990
Highest Honors: Corporations
Honors: Criminal Procedure
Evidence
Federal Taxation

Hastings Communications & Entertainment Law Journal
Executive Notes Editor: 1989 academic year
Staff Writer: 1988 academic year
Journal Note: Topic - Admissibility of Tape Recordings

Undergraduate: **UNIVERSITY OF WASHINGTON**
Seattle, Washington
Awarded Bachelor of Arts in Economics with an emphasis in Political
Science in May 1987
Honors: Distinguished Scholar: 1 semester.
Dean's List: 4 semesters

EMPLOYMENT

DAVIS WRIGHT TREMAINE
Seattle, Washington
Law Clerk/Attorney: Summer 1988; Summer 1989; and Fall 1990 to Present.
Responsible Attorney and Reference: Ronald C. Sullivan, Esq. (206) 666-2343
Significant Work Experience: Assisted JENNIFER KRANOWER, ESQ. in family
law trial in State Court; Attended arbitration for which I had drafted the
brief; Drafting of pretrial documents, arbitration briefs and motions;
Drafting of legal memoranda re: civil and appellate procedure, contract
law, international law (letters rogatory and foreign enforcement of
domestic judgments), professional responsibility, real estate law, tort
law; Extensive research and analysis for RONALD SULLIVAN, ESQ., a
member of the Business Law Section of the State Bar, which is considering
new legislation for Subchapter S corporations.

ADAMS, DUQUE & HAZELTINE
San Francisco, California
Law Clerk: Summer 1987
Responsible Attorney and Reference: Sanford Robitaille, Esq. (415) 643-8989
Significant Work Product Included: Drafting of various legal memoranda.
Offer to return extended.

OTHER EMPLOYMENT: Independent Computer Consultant providing litigation,
transactional and research support for the San Francisco law firms of Bradley
& Curley; Bronson, Bronson & McKinnon; and Bushnell, Caplan & Fielding:
1987-1990.

ADMISSIONS State Bar of Washington.

ADDITIONAL
REFERENCES

PAUL PLOKOWSKY   TERRENCE WALKER   GEORGE BALL
Prof. of Law   Prof. of Law   Prof. of Law
Hastings School of Law   Hastings School of Law   Hastings School of Law
(415) 768-4567   (415) 768-4567   (415) 768-4567

Resume 11—Analysis

1. This resume has a distracting format. The inconsistency in the size of the print makes it difficult to read. Keep your resume uniform, so that the form becomes an invisible vehicle for presenting the information. The content of your resume should draw the reader's attention, not the form.

2. It is unnecessary to include "Esq." after your name. It is presumed that you are an attorney.

3. The Education paragraph is formatted incorrectly. Since it is commonly understood which degree is graduate and which is undergraduate, it is unnecessary to include a subheading or to state that your Juris Doctorate and Bachelor of Arts were "awarded." The attorney, in this example, does not provide her class standing or rank at Hastings College of the Law. Instead, she indicates "honors" in course study. Unless an American Jurisprudence Award or other honorary designation has been awarded, these honor courses should be excluded. A potential employer is more interested to know what your final class standing was than what your individual class achievements were. In any event, a transcript will indicate the classes in which you received high grades. The *Hastings Communications & Entertainment Law Journal* entry should not be separated from the Hastings College of the Law entry and should appear in normal print style. The positions held at the *Journal* should remain noted with only the year; for example, "Executive Notes Editor, 1989." There is no need to include the phrase "academic year." The Journal Note should be specifically named along with the volume and page number in proper footnote form. The undergraduate entry is also incomplete. First, Ms. Change has failed to provide her grade-point average. Second, it is unnecessary to indicate the month of graduation, unless it is an unusual time of year.

4. The Employment section is formatted incorrectly. First, the dates of employment should appear flush to the left margin. Second, it is unnecessary and ill-advised to include the name and phone number of the responsible attorney/reference. Third, the different sizes of print and the capital letters are inappropriate and unprofessional. Fourth, the use of the first person, "I," is an inappropriate way to describe your legal experience. Fifth, the phrase "Offer to return extended" may be simply stated as "Offer extended."

5. The Other Employment as an independent computer consultant is unrelated to the practice of law, even though the employment was with law firms. This is nonlegal employment and should be excluded from your attorney resume.

6. The Admissions paragraph omits the date of admission to the State Bar of Washington.

7. The Additional References section is inappropriate for several significant reasons. First, the names, addresses, and phone numbers of references should never appear within the resume. However, even if these references were intended references by this attorney, they fail for other reasons. The references are all professors at Hastings College of the Law. There is nothing inherently wrong with this; however, the attorney is a 1990 graduate. Ms. Chang has practiced several years. The references of law professors are attenuated in value compared with the more recent reference of an employer. Furthermore, throughout Ms. Chang's resume, she names seven possible attorneys to contact as potential references. As we have discussed, "more is not always better." Again, use your discretion regarding reference providers and never state the names of attorneys for whom you have worked or provide their phone numbers within the body of your resume. Simply use the sentence, "References Available Upon Request."

BENTLEY H. CALDWELL
1989 Rosebush Street, No.34
Washington, DC.20006
(202)   788-9484

OBJECTIVE   TO OBTAIN A LITIGATION ASSOCIATE POSITION WITH A LAW FIRM.

REASON FOR LEAVING   BILLABLE HOURS REQUIREMENTS WERE UNREASONABLE, HAD
                                       PERSONALITY CONFLICT WITH SUPERVISING PARTNER, AND
                                       NO BONUSES GIVEN THIS YEAR.

PROFESSIONAL
EXPERIENCE   LITIGATION. PREPARES MOTIONS, PLEADINGS, DISCOVERY,
                                       MEMORANDA OF POINTS AND AUTHORITIES, RESEARCHES ISSUES
                                       OF LAW AND ATTENDS HEARINGS.

EDUCATION   J.D. 1992, UNIVERSITY OF WISCONSIN, MADISON, WISCONSIN
                                       CLASS RANK: TOP 15%

                                       B.A. 1989, MIDDLEBURY COLLEGE, MIDDLEBURY, VERMONT
                                       MAJOR: ENGLISH
                                       G.P.A. 3.96/4.0

EMPLOYMENT

Sept. 1992 to Present   PEACHTREE, APPLEBLOSSOM & NECTAR
                                       WASHINGTON, DC
                                       ASSOCIATE.

Summer 1991   CARTER, ROOSEVELT & CLINTON
                                       WASHINGTON, DC
                                       LAW CLERK.
                                       RECEIVED OFFER.

ADMISSIONS   WISCONSIN, 1992; DISTRICT OF COLUMBIA, 1992.

LANGUAGES   FRENCH, RUSSIAN.

PERSONAL INTERESTS   GOLF, BASKETBALL, AND JOGGING.

REFERENCES   AVAILABLE UPON REQUEST.

Resume 12—Analysis

1. The format of this resume is distracting. The information appears in all capital letters, except for the dates of employment. The categorical headings are in unprofessional font form.

2. The Objective statement is the most overused and ineffective way to communicate the position you are seeking. Try to include this information in your cover letter.

3. The Reason for Leaving section is unprofessional and inappropriate. Never include your reasons for leaving your present employment in your resume. This is a delicate subject and should be addressed, if asked of you, during an interview.

4. The Professional Experience information is adequate; however, the capital letters are distracting. Furthermore, using upper and lower case letters would allow the author to capitalize the area of practice ("LITIGATION") making it stand out.

5. The Education paragraph is incorrectly formatted. The law school entry fails to include significant information. The complete name of the law school is University of Wisconsin-Madison Law School, and the words "Class Rank" should be underlined, to draw attention to this information. The law school entry information should appear in four lines, with the name of the law school on the first line, the city and state of the law school on the second line, the J.D. degree and graduation year on the third line, and the class rank information on the fourth line. The undergraduate information is formatted poorly as well. The acronym G.P.A. should be underlined to draw attention to it. This entry should appear in four lines: the college name on the first line; the city and state of the college on the second line; the B.A. degree, year, and major on the third line; and the G.P.A. on the fourth line.

6. In the Employment section, the dates of employment should not be abbreviated. The month (September) should be spelled out. The position held should be underlined, and the employment entry should appear in upper and lower case bold letters. Instead of the phrase "Received offer," the resume should state "Offer extended."

7. The Admissions paragraph is correct; however, for simplicity and conformity it should be restated: State Bars of Wisconsin and District of Columbia, 1992.

8. The Languages paragraph should read: Fluent in French and Russian.

9. The References heading is unnecessary. Simply state "References Available Upon Request."

8

Well-Written
Sample Resumes

Over the years, we have drafted many resumes for attorney candidates seeking new employment. As a result, we are keenly aware of how properly constructed and well-organized resumes receive positive attention from prospective employers. As part of our effort to guide you in creating a concise, yet focused resume, we have provided sample resumes in several practice areas. Each resume is uniquely different in what may appear first or last; however, each follows the guidelines discussed throughout this book.

Carefully review the examples when you draft your resume.

The following sample resumes will assist you in preparing your resume.

ROBERT CHASEN
2345 White Oak Avenue
Encino, California
(818) 346-7861

PROFESSIONAL EXPERIENCE:	<u>ACCOUNTANT MALPRACTICE.</u> Research and draft motions, pleadings and memoranda of law. Conduct trial examination, trial brief and jury instructions. Take and defend depositions, argue motions.

EDUCATION:

Duke University School of Law
Durham, North Carolina
J.D. 1989
<u>Class Rank:</u> #12 in the class
Note and Comment Editor, <u>Duke Law Journal</u>

Claremont McKenna College
Claremont, California
B.A. *summa cum laude*, History, 1986

EMPLOYMENT:

September 1989 to Present
Brobeck, Phleger & Harrison
Los Angeles, California
<u>Associate.</u>

Summer 1988
Dewey Ballantine
Los Angeles, California
<u>Summer Associate.</u> Offer extended.

BAR ADMISSION: State Bar of California, 1989.

PERSONAL INTERESTS: Sailing.

REFERENCES AVAILABLE UPON REQUEST

JOHN PARLUCCI
426 Hudson Street
Hackensack, New Jersey   07601
(201)   342-3906

EDUCATION:	**Rutgers University/Newark School of Law** Newark, New Jersey J.D. *summa cum laude*, 1989 Class Rank: Top 5%
	Bowdoin College Brunswick, Maine B.A. *cum laude*, English, 1986
EMPLOYMENT:	
March 1992 to Present	**Breslin & Breslin, P.A.** Hackensack, New Jersey Accountant Malpractice Litigation Associate. Complex accountant malpractice litigation and FSLIC/FDIC claims of director and officer liability. Responsibilities include assistance in case management and strategy formulation, extensive investigation, discovery, interaction with experts, research, and writing.
September 1989 to February 1992; Summer 1988	**Berlin, Kaplan, Dembling & Burke** Hackensack, New Jersey Accountant and Legal Malpractice Litigation Associate.
BAR ADMISSION:	State Bar of New Jersey, 1989; Admitted to U.S. District Court, District of New Jersey, 1990.
PERSONAL INTERESTS:	Basketball and golf.

REFERENCES AVAILABLE UPON REQUEST

CHARLES SULLIVAN
850 Pine Street
New York, New York   10038
(212)   777-4980

EDUCATION:

Howard University School of Law
Washington, D.C.
J.D. 1992
Class Rank: Top 15%
Note & Comment Editor, Howard Law Review

Hofstra University
Hempstead, New York
B.A. *magna cum laude,* Economics, 1989
G.P.A.: 3.8/4.0

EMPLOYMENT:

October 1992
to Present

Maritime Overseas Corporation
New York, New York
Maritime Attorney. Responsible for legal services for vessel
design, construction, financing, and chartering for large container
shipping company. Set up and arrange government financing and
approvals for company that constructs and operates feeder vessel.

Summer 1991

Honorable Chester Woodbridge
U.S. District Court, Eastern District of New York
Extern.

**BAR ADMISSION
& ACTIVITIES:**

State Bar of New York, 1992; Member, Maritime Law Association
of the United States.

PERSONAL INTERESTS: Sailing and windsurfing.

REFERENCES AVAILABLE UPON REQUEST

RICHARD P. DUFFY
5472 West Glenbury Road
Pasadena, California 91101
(818) 793-4523

EDUCATION:

University of Iowa College of Law
Iowa City, Iowa
J.D. 1989
Order of the Coif
Note & Comment Editor, <u>Iowa Law Review</u>

Iowa State University
Ames, Iowa
B.A. *summa cum laude,* English, 1986
<u>G.P.A.:</u> 4.0/4.0

EMPLOYMENT:

September 1989
to Present;
Summer 1988

Gibson, Dunn & Crutcher
Los Angeles, California
<u>Appellate Litigation Associate</u>. Involved in several insurance
matters including coverage disputes, bad faith claims,
alleged errors or omissions on part of insurance agents, products
liability, and legal malpractice. Take and defend depositions.
Draft and argue motions. Draft trial briefs.

Summer 1987

Honorable Catherine Vigil
Iowa City Superior Court Appellate Department
<u>Extern</u>.

BAR ADMISSION
& ACTIVITIES:

State Bar of California, 1989; The American Academy of
Appellate Lawyers.

PERSONAL INTERESTS: Creative writing.

REFERENCES AVAILABLE UPON REQUEST

McNALLY DOUGLAS
501 Dakota Avenue
New York, New York   10166
(212)   351-4223

PROFESSIONAL EXPERIENCE:	BANKRUPTCY LITIGATION PRACTICE. Research and draft motions, pleadings, and memoranda of law. Participate in arbitration proceedings. Argue motions in Bankruptcy Court. Take and defend depositions. Conduct client interviews.

EMPLOYMENT:

September 1993 to Present	**Gibson, Dunn & Crutcher** New York, New York Associate.
Summer 1992	**Cleary, Gottlieb, Steen & Hamilton** New York, New York Summer Associate. Offer extended.
Summer 1991	**New York City Department of Law, Office of the Corporation Counsel** New York, New York Summer Intern in the Family Court Division.
EDUCATION:	**Fordham University** New York, New York J.D. 1993 Class Rank: #5 in the class Note and Comment Editor, Fordham Law Review
	Colgate University Hamilton, New York B.S. *magna cum laude*, Mathematics, 1990
BAR ADMISSION & ACTIVITIES:	State Bar of New York, 1993. Member, Association of the Bar of the City of New York (Member, Committee on Bankruptcy and Corporate Reorganization).
PERSONAL INTERESTS:	Racquetball and backpacking.

REFERENCES AVAILABLE UPON REQUEST

MERLE FISHMAN
33 Oliver Street
Boston, Massachusetts 02109
(617) 428-8359

EDUCATION: **Boston University School of Law**
Boston, Massachusetts
J.D. 1990
Class Rank: Top 15%
Member, Boston University Law Review

Boston College
Newton, Massachusetts
B.A. *summa cum laude,* Art History, 1987
G.P.A.: 4.0/4.0

EMPLOYMENT:

September 1990 **Bingham, Dana & Gould**
to Present Boston, Massachusetts
Bankruptcy Litigation Associate. Involved in complex bankruptcy and commercial litigation matters. Primary responsibility for business bankruptcy proceedings and workouts. Draft pleadings and discovery papers, argue motions, research and draft memoranda of law, review and analyze commercial documents, and conduct settlement negotiations. Draft and negotiate various commercial transactions.

Summer 1989 **Assistant District Attorney**
Suffolk County District Attorney's Office
Extern.

BAR ADMISSION State Bar of Massachusetts, 1990; American Bar Association;
& ACTIVITIES: Fellow: American College of Trial Lawyers; Vice-President, Boston Bar Association.

PERSONAL INTERESTS: Water skiing, Russian literature, and French cooking.

REFERENCES AVAILABLE UPON REQUEST

JOHN SCHMIDT
820 Second Avenue
Seattle, Washington 98101
(206) 871-1213

EMPLOYMENT:

September 1991
to Present;
Summer 1990

Bogle & Gates
Seattle, Washington
Bankruptcy Litigation Associate. Involved in complex bankruptcy matters. Primary responsibility for business bankruptcy proceedings and workouts. Draft pleadings and discovery papers, argue motions, research and draft memoranda of law, review and analyze commercial documents, and conduct settlement negotiations.

EDUCATION:

University of Michigan Law School
Ann Arbor, Michigan
J.D. 1991
Class Rank: Top Third

Willamette University
Salem, Washington
B.A. *magna cum laude,* Political Science, 1988
G.P.A.: 3.9/4.0

BAR ADMISSION: State Bar of Washington, 1991.

PERSONAL INTERESTS: Sailing and tennis.

REFERENCES AVAILABLE UPON REQUEST

ALLAN CARSON
3489 Peach Street
Hartford, Connecticut   06101
(203)   728-8392

EMPLOYMENT:

April 1990
to Present

United Technologies Corporation
Hartford, Connecticut
Senior Counsel. Responsible for all workouts and workout strategies and review debtor business plans. Develop strategies for maintaining collateral value, devise business alternatives for foreclosed businesses and create and implement plans to sell or liquidate foreclosed businesses and assets. Structure standard terms and conditions for documentation of commercial and consumer loans, including inventory finance, asset-based lending, equipment finance and leasing, real estate and capital loans, structured joint ventures, equity participations, and stock and asset acquisitions and divestitures. Develop business plans, make short-term and long-term operating decisions.

September 1986
to March 1990;
Summer 1985

Reid & Reige, P.C.
Hartford, Connecticut
Bankruptcy Associate.

EDUCATION:

University of Connecticut School of Law
Hartford, Connecticut
J.D. 1986
Class Rank: Approximately Top 15%
Member, Connecticut Law Review

Northeastern University
Boston, Massachusetts
B.A. *cum laude*, Political Science, 1983
G.P.A.: 3.6/4.0

BAR ADMISSION: State Bar of Connecticut, 1986.

PERSONAL INTERESTS: Cross-country and downhill skiing.

REFERENCES AVAILABLE UPON REQUEST

DAVID BENJAMIN MONKARSH
13812 Rosebury Lane
Chicago, Illinois 60603
(312)   845-7869

PROFESSIONAL EXPERIENCE:	BANKRUPTCY PRACTICE. Involves primarily insolvency and workout matters and secondarily business litigation. Handle debtor and creditor matters. Represent real estate mortgage company as Chapter 11 debtor in possession, retail company in disputes involving its commercial leases of 23 retail outlets to Chapter 11 debtor in possession and represent credit corporation as plaintiff in an adversary proceeding against financial institution as indenture trustee, seeking to enforce subordination provisions in a "junk bond" indenture agreement issued prior to bankruptcy by Chapter 11 debtor.

EMPLOYMENT:

April 1990 to Present	**Chapman & Cutler** Chicago, Illinois Bankruptcy Of Counsel.
September 1982 to March 1990; Summer 1981	**Gardner, Catron & Douglas** Chicago, Illinois Bankruptcy Associate.

EDUCATION:	**Harvard University Law School** Cambridge, Massachusetts J.D. 1982 Class Rank: Approximately Top 15% Member, Harvard Law Review
	University of Chicago Chicago, Illinois B.A. *summa cum laude*, Political Science, 1979 G.P.A.: 4.0/4.0 Phi Beta Kappa

BAR ADMISSION:	State Bar of Illinois, 1982.

PERSONAL INTERESTS:	Basketball and swimming.

REFERENCES AVAILABLE UPON REQUEST

SHARON PETERMAN
2390 East 72nd Street
New York, New York 10019
(212)   373-1241

EDUCATION:

University of Chicago Law School
Chicago, Illinois
J.D. 1991
Order of the Coif
Class Rank: Approximately Top 5%

Columbia University
New York, New York
B.A. *summa cum laude*, English, 1988
G.P.A.: 4.0/4.0
Phi Beta Kappa

EMPLOYMENT:

November 1991
to Present;
Summer 1990

Paul, Weiss, Rifkind, Wharton & Garrison
New York, New York
Bankruptcy Associate. Involves primarily insolvency and workout matters and secondarily business litigation. Handle debtor and creditor matters. Represent real estate mortgage company as Chapter 11 debtor in possession, retail company in disputes involving its commercial leases of 23 retail outlets to Chapter 11 debtor in possession and represent credit corporation as plaintiff in an adversary proceeding against financial institution as indenture trustee, seeking to enforce subordination provisions in a "junk bond" indenture agreement issued prior to bankruptcy by Chapter 11 debtor.

Summer 1990

Phillips, Nizer, Benjamin, Krim & Ballon
New York, New York
Summer Associate. Offer extended.

BAR ADMISSION: State Bar of New York, 1991.

PERSONAL INTERESTS: Modern dance and jazz.

REFERENCES AVAILABLE UPON REQUEST

RONALD E. SCOTT
2400 Pico Boulevard, Apt. 415
Los Angeles, California 90064
(310) 395-6718

PROFESSIONAL EXPERIENCE:	<u>BANKRUPTCY PRACTICE.</u> Involves primarily insolvency and workout matters and secondarily business litigation. Handle debtor and creditor matters. Represent real estate mortgage company as Chapter 11 debtor in possession, retail company in disputes involving its commercial leases of 23 retail outlets to Chapter 11 debtor in possession and represent credit corporation as plaintiff in an adversary proceeding against financial institution as indenture trustee, seeking to enforce subordination provisions in a "junk bond" indenture agreement issued prior to bankruptcy by Chapter 11 debtor.
EDUCATION:	**New York University School of Law** New York, New York J.D. 1988 <u>Class Rank:</u> Approximately Top 10% **Rutgers University** Newark, New Jersey B.A. *summa cum laude*, History, 1985 <u>G.P.A.:</u> 4.0/4.0 Phi Beta Kappa

EMPLOYMENT:

Fall 1990 to Present	**Stutman, Treister & Glatt** Los Angeles, California <u>Bankruptcy Associate.</u>
November 1988 to December 1989; Summer 1987	**Gibson, Dunn & Crutcher** Los Angeles, California <u>Bankruptcy Associate.</u>

BAR ADMISSION:	State Bar of California, 1988.
PERSONAL INTERESTS:	Baseball, golf, and skiing.

REFERENCES AVAILABLE UPON REQUEST

ARTHUR BRADY
9658 West Fifth Street
Cleveland, Ohio 44114
(216) 696-8375

EMPLOYMENT:

November 1992 to Present	**Jones, Day, Reavis & Pogue** Cleveland, Ohio Civil Litigation Associate. Practice includes law and motion work and all aspects of discovery. Draft legal memoranda, opinion letters, and briefs concerning a variety of issues in wrongful termination and general contract law. Draft various contract provisions, demand letters, and settlement agreements.
October 1990 to October 1992; Summer 1989	**Arter & Hadden** Cleveland, Ohio Litigation Associate.
Summer 1988	**Federal Trade Commission** Washington, DC Summer Extern.

EDUCATION:

Case Western Reserve University School of Law
Cleveland, Ohio
J.D. 1990
Class Rank: Top 15%
Honors: American Jurisprudence Award in Torts.

University of North Carolina at Greensboro
Greensboro, North Carolina
M.A. Economics, 1986
G.P.A.: 3.8/4.0

Ohio State University
Columbus, Ohio
B.S. *summa cum laude*, Economics, 1985

BAR ADMISSION: State Bar of Ohio, 1990. Admitted to practice in the U.S. District Court, Northern District of Ohio.

REFERENCES AVAILABLE UPON REQUEST

Civil Litigation Resume

RALPH W. PICK
372 Capitol Drive
Sacramento, California   95814
(916)   774-9177

PROFESSIONAL EXPERIENCE:

<u>CIVIL LITIGATION PRACTICE.</u> Draft and argue various motions and pleadings in Federal and State court. Prepare and draft interrogatories, document requests, and answer same. Prepare and draft summary judgment motions, discovery motions, and motions to compel. Research and draft memoranda. Write opinion letters to clients. Significant client contact.

EDUCATION:

University of California, at Berkeley
Boalt Hall
Berkeley, California
J.D. 1992
Order of the Coif
Note and Comment Editor, <u>California Law Review</u>

Massachusetts Institute of Technology
Cambridge, Massachusetts
B.S. *magna cum laude*, Mathematics, 1989

EMPLOYMENT:

September 1992
to Present

Orrick, Herrington & Sutcliffe
Sacramento, California
<u>Associate.</u>

Summer 1991

Pettit & Martin
San Francisco, California
<u>Summer Associate.</u> Offer extended.

Summer 1990

Honorable Randall Wonderville
U.S. Court of Appeals, Ninth Circuit Court
<u>Extern.</u>

BAR ADMISSION & ACTIVITIES:

State Bar of California, 1992. Admitted to U.S. District Court, Southern District, Central District and U.S. Court of Appeals, Ninth District. State Bar Association (Member, Litigation Section).

PERSONAL INTERESTS: Football, handball, and golf.

REFERENCES AVAILABLE UPON REQUEST

DOROTHY SILVERSTEIN
1234 Fifth Avenue
New York, New York 10004
(212) 746-2776

PROFESSIONAL EXPERIENCE:	<u>CIVIL LITIGATION PRACTICE.</u> Responsible for own case load, from inception through trial. Draft and argue pretrial and discovery motions in federal and state court. Prepare and draft interrogatories, document requests, and answer same. Take and defend depositions, prepare legal memoranda and discovery documents. Draft opinion letters and briefs. Draft demand letters and settlement agreements.

EMPLOYMENT:

August 1992 to Present	**Fried, Frank, Harris, Shriver & Jacobson** New York, New York <u>Litigation Associate.</u>
August 1988 to July 1992; Summer 1987	**Jones, Day, Reavis & Pogue** Cleveland, Ohio <u>Litigation Associate.</u>

EDUCATION:	**Cornell University Law School** Ithaca, New York J.D. 1988 <u>Class Rank:</u> Top 25%
	Wheaton College Norton, Massachusetts B.A. *magna cum laude*, Political Science, 1985

BAR ADMISSIONS:	State Bars of Ohio, 1988; New York, 1992. U.S. District Court, Northern District of Ohio; New York and U.S. District Court, Southern and Eastern Districts of New York.

PERSONAL INTERESTS:	Bicycling and aerobics.

REFERENCES AVAILABLE UPON REQUEST

SAMUEL R. PRESTONE
3221 Cadillac Avenue
Chicago, Illinois 60605
(312) 765-4321

PROFESSIONAL
EXPERIENCE:

<u>COMMERCIAL LITIGATION PRACTICE.</u> Representation of financial institutions. Conduct discovery, take and defend depositions, draft a variety of pleadings and pretrial motions, and regularly appear in court on law and motion, writs and receivers, and default prove-up calendars. Responsible for own case load, negotiate settlements, and have extensive client contact.

EDUCATION:

Georgetown University Law Center
Georgetown, Washington, DC
J.D. 1989
<u>Class Rank:</u> Top 6%
<u>Honors</u>: American Jurisprudence Award for International Tax

University of Michigan
Ann Arbor, Michigan
A.B. with high distinction, Economics, 1986
Phi Beta Kappa

EMPLOYMENT:

November 1991
to Present

Mayer, Brown & Platt
Chicago, Illinois
<u>Associate.</u>

April 1990
to October 1991

Lord, Bissell & Brook
Chicago, Illinois
<u>Associate.</u>

September 1989
to March 1990;
Summer 1988

Sonnenschein, Nath & Rosenthal
Chicago, Illinois
<u>Associate.</u>

BAR ADMISSION:

State Bar of Illinois, 1989.

REFERENCES AVAILABLE UPON REQUEST

WALTER K. WESTERBERRY
4561 Queensbridge Road, Apt. 760
Cincinnati, Ohio 45202
(513)   579-3678

EMPLOYMENT:

March 1983
to Present

American Financial Corporation
Cincinnati, Ohio
Senior Counsel. Report to General Counsel. Responsible for litigation supervision and client advice on broad range of general commercial litigation matters. Responsibilities include supervision of commercial litigation, creditor bankruptcy and credit matters. Interface with outside counsel.

September 1980
to February 1983;
Summer 1979

Reisenfeld & Associates
Cincinnati, Ohio
Commercial Litigation Associate.

EDUCATION:

Ohio Northern University,
Claude W. Pettit College of Law
Ada, Ohio
J.D. 1980
Class Rank: Top Third

Ohio State University
Columbus, Ohio
B.A. English, 1977
G.P.A.: 3.45/4.0

BAR ADMISSION: State Bar of Ohio, 1980.

PERSONAL INTERESTS: Bowling.

REFERENCES AVAILABLE UPON REQUEST

JACOB B. ZIMMERMAN
12 Charles Place
New York, New York 10022
(212) 349-3419

EDUCATION:

State University of New York, at Buffalo School of Law
Buffalo, New York
J.D. 1993
Class Standing: #1 in the class
Editor, Buffalo Law Review
Honors: American Jurisprudence Awards in Real Property,
Contracts, Evidence, Civil Procedure, Torts, Corporations.

Hofstra University
Hempstead, New York
B.A. *cum laude*, English, 1990

EMPLOYMENT:

November 1993
to Present;
Summer 1992

Baker & McKenzie
New York, New York
Commercial Litigation Associate. Representation of financial
institutions. Conduct discovery, take and defend depositions, draft
variety of pleadings and pretrial motions, and appear in court on
law and motion, writs and receivers, and default prove-up
calendars. Responsible for own case load, negotiate settlements,
and have extensive client contact.

Summer 1991

Honorable Patricia Howgood
U.S. District Court, Northern District of New York
Extern.

BAR ADMISSION: State Bar of New York, 1993.

PERSONAL INTERESTS: Weight training, snow skiing, and basketball.

REFERENCES AVAILABLE UPON REQUEST

JOHN ADAMS
5201 Shell Street
Houston, Texas 77002
(713) 228-9724

PROFESSIONAL
EXPERIENCE:

<u>CONSTRUCTION DEFECT LITIGATION PRACTICE.</u> All aspects of construction litigation practice including legal research, drafting and arguing motions, developing discovery plans, taking and defending depositions, preparation of evidence, and exhibits for trial. Negotiate and draft settlement agreements, conduct arbitrations, participated as second chair in trial. Full responsibility over assigned cases.

EDUCATION:

Vanderbilt University School of Law
Nashville, Tennessee
J.D. 1988
<u>Class Rank:</u> #10 in the class
<u>Honors:</u> American Jurisprudence Awards in Real Property, Torts and Trial Practice; Quarterfinalist in Advocacy Tournament (1987), Top First Tier Moot Court Brief.

University of Texas
Austin, Texas
B.A. *magna cum laude*, Philosophy, 1985
Phi Beta Kappa

EMPLOYMENT:

October 1988
to Present

Fulbright & Jaworski
Houston, Texas
<u>Associate.</u>

Summer 1987

Jenkins & Gilchrist
Houston, Texas
<u>Summer Associate.</u> Offer extended.

BAR ADMISSION
& ACTIVITIES:

State Bar of Texas, 1988; American Bar Association, Texas Trial Lawyers Association.

PERSONAL INTERESTS: Camping and fishing.

REFERENCES AVAILABLE UPON REQUEST

Construction Litigation Resume

DAVID HO
1717 Dove Avenue
Newport Beach, California   92660
(714)   852-2690

EMPLOYMENT:

October 1990
to Present;
Summer 1989

McKittrick, Jackson, DeMarco & Peckenpaugh
Newport Beach, California
Construction Litigation Associate. Practice includes legal
research, drafting and arguing motions, developing discovery
plans, taking and defending depositions, prepare evidence
and exhibits for trial, negotiate and draft settlement agreements.

Summer 1988

District Attorney's Office
Fourth Judicial District of Utah
Extern.

EDUCATION:

Brigham Young University, J. Reuben Clark Law School
Provo, Utah
J.D. *cum laude*, 1990
Note and Comment Editor, Brigham Young University Law Review

San Francisco State University
San Francisco, California
B.A. *cum laude*, English, 1987
G.P.A.: 3.6/4.0

BAR ADMISSION:

State Bar of California, 1991.

LANGUAGE:

Fluent in Mandarin Chinese.

PERSONAL INTERESTS:

Golf, tennis, and skiing.

REFERENCES AVAILABLE UPON REQUEST

WANDA ALLEN
110 West Summit Drive
Knoxville, Tennessee 37901-2649
(615) 637-8533

EDUCATION:

University of California, at Berkeley
Boalt Hall
Berkeley, California
J.D. 1987
Class Standing: Top 10%
Honors: American Jurisprudence Awards: Real Property,
Corporations and Remedies.

University of California, Santa Cruz
Santa Cruz, California
B.A. 1984, English

EMPLOYMENT:

August 1990
to Present

Baker, Worthington, Crossley, Stansbury & Woolf
Knoxville, Tennessee
Senior Corporate Associate. Alternative Energy Project Finance
Emphasis. Negotiate and draft power sales contracts; design,
engineering, and construction contracts; operating and
maintenance contracts; and partnership agreements in connection
with the development of small power production facilities and
cogeneration facilities. Draft asset purchase agreements in
connection with acquisition of several existing cogeneration
facilities. Draft various petitions before the Federal Energy
Regulatory Commission and several state public utility
commissions; and represent investment banks in connection with
leveraged leases of enhanced oil recovery facility and geothermal
small power production facility.

September 1987
to July 1990;
Summer 1986

Brobeck, Phleger & Harrison
San Francisco, California
Corporate Associate. Negotiated and drafted loan agreements,
promissory notes, and ancillary documents in connection with real
estate loans; represented public companies in connection with
preparation of Forms 10-Q, 10-K, and 8-K and Registration
Statements in connection with exchange offer and initial public
offering; and assisted in due diligence for a leveraged buyout; and
drafted various other documents including asset purchase
agreements, employment agreements, and stock option plans.

Summer 1985

Honorable Walter Prescott, Jr.
United States District Court for the Central District of California
Extern.

BAR ADMISSIONS: State Bars of California, 1987; Tennessee, 1990.

PERSONAL INTERESTS: Compose guitar music.

REFERENCES AVAILABLE UPON REQUEST

GEORGE BROOM
140 Peach Avenue
Atlanta, Georgia 30303
(404) 885-0990

EMPLOYMENT:

October 1987
to Present;
Summer 1986

Paul, Hastings, Janofsky & Walker
Atlanta, Georgia
Corporate/Banking Associate. Substantial transactional
experience representing major corporations, investment bankers
and advisors, and investors. Transactional experience includes
mergers and acquisitions, defensive and offensive takeover work,
corporate restructurings and recapitalizations, and public and
private offerings (including letter of credit-backed floating rate
notes and convertible debt offerings). Substantial transactional
and regulatory experience primarily representing underwriters,
savings and loan associations, national banks, and state-chartered
banks. Experience includes sales of assets, securities offerings
(including subordinated debt offerings, underwritten CD offerings
and conversions).

EDUCATION:

University of California, Los Angeles School of Law
Los Angeles, California
J.D. 1987
Class Rank: Approximately Top 11%

Atlanta University
Atlanta, Georgia
B.A. *summa cum laude*, Political Science, 1984
Phi Beta Kappa

BAR ADMISSION:

State Bar of Georgia, 1987.

PERSONAL INTERESTS:

Water skiing and gardening.

REFERENCES AVAILABLE UPON REQUEST

Corporate/Banking Resume

SUSAN HALLQUIST
501 North Holt Avenue
Harrisburg, Pennsylvania   17108
(717)   553-2012

**PROFESSIONAL
EXPERIENCE:**

CORPORATE/FINANCE PRACTICE. Specialize in financing transactions, including representation of commercial banks and finance companies in negotiating and documenting lease financings of equipment, secured and unsecured lending transactions, interest rate swaps and ship mortgages and representation of corporate clients in connection with leveraged buyout financings and stock and asset purchase and sale transactions.

EDUCATION:

Harvard University Law School
Cambridge, Massachusetts
J.D. 1989
Class Rank: Top 25%

University of Pennsylvania
Philadelphia, Pennsylvania
B.A. *summa cum laude*, Economics, 1986

EMPLOYMENT:

October 1992
to Present

Schnader, Harrison, Segal & Lewis
Harrisburg, Pennsylvania
Associate.

October 1990
to September 1992

Stroock & Stroock & Lavan
New York, New York
Associate.

October 1989
to September 1990;
Summer 1988

Shearman & Sterling
New York, New York
Associate.

BAR ADMISSIONS:

State Bars of New York, 1989; Pennsylvania, 1992.

LANGUAGE:

Fluent in Mandarin Chinese.

REFERENCES AVAILABLE UPON REQUEST

KATHERINE HEIDEL
1602 North Beach
San Francisco, California 97346
(415) 563-0140

EDUCATION:

Columbia University School of Law
New York, New York
J.D. 1986
Class Standing: Top Third

Barnard College
New York, New York
B.A. *magna cum laude*, English, 1983

EMPLOYMENT:

June 1992
to Present

Bank of America
San Francisco, California
Assistant General Counsel. Responsible for all aspects of in-house banking regulatory practice, including drafting applications, correspondence, and memoranda regarding expanded powers, regulatory compliance, insurance and bond underwriting, investment securities, acquisitions, mergers, consolidations and reorganizations, charter conversions, branching, deposit insurance, asset management, leasing, data processing, real estate investment and development, political action committees and federal and state election laws and regulations, new products, and international activities. Author comment letters on regulatory proposals including personal property appraisals, payments systems operations, reserve requirements, and highly leveraged transactions. Advise in-house clients on all regulatory matters. Interact with Federal Reserve, OCC, FDIC, OTS, FFIEC, RTC, and several state banking authorities. Develop bylaws and articles of association for new bank subsidiary. Regularly summarize pending regulatory proposals and proposed banking legislation.

September 1987
to May 1992

Board of Governors of the Federal Reserve System
Washington, DC
Staff Attorney. Researched and drafted legal memoranda, Board regulations and correspondence on a variety of monetary and banking issues including: payment systems, reserve requirements, Competitive Equality Banking Act, Financial Institutions Reform, Recovery and Enforcement Act, Federal Reserve membership applications; and administrative issues, including organizational issues for Oversight Board, Right to Financial Privacy Act, Trade Secrets Act, money laundering legislation, and currency queries. Drafted and coordinated Board's proposed revision of Regulation J, Subpart B - Funds Transfers Through Fedwire, to make it consistent with Article 4A of UCC.

September 1986 to August 1987; Summer 1985	**Dewey, Cheatem & Howe** (Dissolution of Firm, July 1987) New York, New York <u>Banking Associate.</u>

BAR ADMISSIONS: State Bars of New York, 1986; District of Columbia, 1987.

PERSONAL INTERESTS: Backpacking, hiking, and photography.

REFERENCES AVAILABLE UPON REQUEST

CHANDLER WOOD, II
777 West Nestle Avenue
Rochester, New York 14652
(716) 724-1634

EDUCATION: Yale University Law School
New Haven, Connecticut
J.D. 1988
Editor, Yale Law Review

Virginia Military Institute
Lexington, Virginia
B.S. *summa cum laude*, Economics, 1985

EMPLOYMENT:

November 1990
to Present

Eastman Kodak Company
Rochester, New York
Corporate/International Attorney. Serve as counsel
for international joint ventures, business dispositions and other
commercial transactions, utilizing experts on negotiation teams.
Organization of multifunctional team in establishing 50/50 joint
venture in new product start-up. Form minority-owned joint
venture, utilizing unrepatriated earnings of Singapore subsidiary.
Divest six businesses, managing all legal issues including
business and antitrust planning, negotiating agreements with
acquiring companies and their financing institutions and
structuring employee and other transitions. Form 50/50 joint
venture market development and distribution company with
Japanese manufacturer. Assure survival of financially weak
critical supplier by negotiating financing agreements with
supplier, his bank, and other stockholders.

September 1988
to October 1990;
Summer 1987

Kaye, Scholer, Fierman, Hays & Handler
New York, New York
Corporate Associate.

BAR ADMISSION: State Bar of New York, 1988.

LANGUAGES: Fluent in Korean, Mandarin Chinese, and Japanese.

PERSONAL INTERESTS: Asian travel and reading biographies.

REFERENCES AVAILABLE UPON REQUEST

SARI GOLDSTEIN
1772 Palisades Drive
Pacific Palisades, California 90272
(310) 471-6778

EDUCATION:

University of Michigan Law School
Ann Arbor, Michigan
J.D. 1991
Class Standing: Top 20%
Associate Editor, Michigan Law Review

Pitzer College
Clairemont, California
B.A. *summa cum laude*, English, 1988

EMPLOYMENT:

August 1991
to Present;
Summer 1990

O'Melveny & Myers
Los Angeles, California
Corporate/Municipal Finance Associate. Practice concentration includes municipal bond issuance and creation of 501(c)(3) corporations. Experience as both underwriter's and bond counsel on Mello-Roos financings, certificate of participation financings, and tax and revenue anticipation notes.

Summer 1989

Justice Oscar Mendoza
Michigan Supreme Court
Intern.

BAR ADMISSION: State Bar of California, 1991.

PERSONAL INTERESTS: Poetry and flute.

REFERENCES AVAILABLE UPON REQUEST

HARRIET JORDAN
710 Harrisburg Avenue
Philadelphia, Pennsylvania 19103
(215) 322-4663

EMPLOYMENT:

October 1992
to Present

Dechert, Price & Rhoads
Philadelphia, Pennsylvania
<u>Tax Associate.</u> Business tax planning including mergers and acquisitions and international transactions; individual, trust, and corporate returns; qualification and return of tax-exempt organizations; deferred compensation arrangements; estate planning; compliance with ERISA; revenue rulings and appellate conferences.

Summer 1991

Ervin, Cohen & Jessup
Beverly Hills, California
<u>Summer Associate.</u> Offer extended.

EDUCATION:

Loyola Marymount University Law School
Los Angeles, California
J.D. 1992
<u>Class Rank:</u> Top 11%
Member, <u>Loyola of Los Angeles Law Review</u>

University of Pennsylvania
Philadelphia, Pennsylvania
B.S. *magna cum laude*, Accounting, 1989

BAR ADMISSION:
State Bar of Pennsylvania, 1992; American Bar Association (Section of Taxation).

PERSONAL INTERESTS: Crossword puzzles.

REFERENCES AVAILABLE UPON REQUEST

DENNIS R. SPENDTHRIFT
233 Cornelius Court
Dallas, Texas 75225
(214) 751-9232

PROFESSIONAL EXPERIENCE:

<u>CORPORATE AND PARTNERSHIP TAX PRACTICE.</u> Experience in tax for foreign and domestic corporations and individuals including planning in response to the Tax Reform Act of 1986, research and draft memoranda of law. Research various U.S. federal and Texas tax laws, and position papers to I.R.S. regarding audits. Draft tax opinion letters regarding acquisition of real property and corporate financing transactions. Research law, consult with foreign counsel and prepare memoranda of law.

EMPLOYMENT:

October 1991 to Present

Akin, Gump, Haver & Feld
Dallas, Texas
<u>Senior Tax Associate.</u>

June 1988 to September 1991

Butler & Binion
Dallas, Texas
<u>Tax Associate.</u>

November 1986 to May 1988; Summer 1985

Fulbright & Jaworski
Dallas, Texas
<u>Tax Associate.</u>

EDUCATION:

University of Texas at Austin School of Law
Austin, Texas
J.D./M.B.A. 1986
<u>J.D. Class Rank:</u> #1 in the class
Note and Comment Editor, <u>Texas Law Review</u>
<u>Honors:</u> First in class of Income Tax I and II, Advanced Business Taxation, Estate and Gift Tax, Estate Planning and Estate and Trusts.

University of Chicago
Chicago, Illinois
B.A. *summa cum laude*, Economics, 1983

BAR ADMISSION AND ACTIVITIES:

State Bar of Texas, 1986; American Bar Association (Section of Taxation, Partnership) Committee, 1987-1993.

PERSONAL INTERESTS: Archery.

REFERENCES AVAILABLE UPON REQUEST

ROBERTA MILLER-SMITH
200 West Madison Street
Chicago, Illinois 60606
(312) 782-1400

PROFESSIONAL EXPERIENCE:	<u>CORPORATE/REAL ESTATE PRACTICE.</u> Drafting of purchase and sale agreements for the acquisition of raw land and commercially developed properties. Negotiation and drafting of shopping center leases, including leases for large retail anchor tenant. Preparation of private placement memoranda and securities filings. Drafting of partnership agreements, joint venture agreements, stock purchase agreements, and shareholder's agreements. Formation of corporations and drafting of all corporate documents including certificates of determination.

EDUCATION:

Yale University Law School
New Haven, Connecticut
J.D. 1986
<u>Honors:</u> Best Oral Argument (Moot Court Competition)

Barnard College
New York, New York
B.A. *magna cum laude*, Economics, 1983

EMPLOYMENT:

January 1989 to Present	**McCormick Foundation** Chicago, Illinois <u>Associate Counsel.</u>
October 1986 to December 1988; Summer 1985	**Landels, Ripley & Diamond** San Francisco, California <u>Real Estate Associate.</u>

BAR ADMISSIONS: State Bars of California, 1986; Illinois, 1988.

PERSONAL INTERESTS: Tennis and aerobics.

REFERENCES AVAILABLE UPON REQUEST

ARMANDO TIMMONS
95 Chesnut Street
Providence, Rhode Island   02903
(401)   361-7682

EDUCATION:

University of Wisconsin-Madison Law School
Madison, Wisconsin
J.D. 1988
Class Rank: Top 10%

University of Washington
Seattle, Washington
B.A. *summa cum laude*, Political Science, 1985

EMPLOYMENT:

January 1989
to Present

Adler, Pollock & Sheehan
Providence, Rhode Island
Corporate/Real Estate Associate. Includes representation of institutional lenders (including preparation and negotiation of loan documentation, title, and survey review); commercial leasing; real property acquisitions; drafting various agreements (including shareholder agreements, voting agreements, whole loan purchase agreements, stock purchase agreements); drafting opinions and conducting due diligence investigations; drafting SEC no-action letter; preparing and filing permit applications for qualification of securities preparing franchise offering circular.

September 1988
to December 1988;
Summer 1987

Ross & Stevens
Madison, Wisconsin
Associate.

BAR ADMISSIONS: State Bars of Wisconsin and Rhode Island, 1988.

PERSONAL INTERESTS: Water skiing and sailing.

REFERENCES AVAILABLE UPON REQUEST

SCOTT AVERY
12 Maple Avenue
Dallas, Texas   75201
(214)   871-9669

PROFESSIONAL
EXPERIENCE:

CORPORATE SECURITIES PRACTICE. Substantial involvement in all aspects of multijurisdictional asset purchase involving seven countries; prepare documents and assist clients with implementing a shareholder rights plan, negotiate merger agreement and related documents in connection with merger of privately held company into subsidiary of public company; prepare S-8 registration statements, New York Stock Exchange Original Listing Application, proxy statements, and private placement memoranda for Regulation D and Regulation S offerings; handle related Blue Sky matters; act as liaison with foreign counsel regarding securities matters; advise clients regarding Section 16(b) short-swing trading rules, including as they relate to employee benefit plans and convertible securities; advise on implementing a short-swing compliance program; negotiate and prepare agreements, including securities purchase agreements for venture capital transactions, shareholders' agreements, employment agreements, stock-option agreements, and licensing agreements; generally familiar with Hart-Scott-Rodino, Exon-Florio, Trust Indenture Act of 1939, Investment Advisors Act of 1940, and broker-dealer regulations. Advise corporate clients in creating a record of good faith in anticipation of minority shareholder lawsuits; and prepare loan documentation.

EDUCATION:

University of Michigan Law School
Ann Arbor, Michigan
J.D. 1989
Class Rank: Top 15%

Southern Methodist University
Dallas, Texas
B.A. *summa cum laude*, Political Science, 1986

EMPLOYMENT:

March 1992
to Present

Andrews & Kurth
Dallas, Texas
Associate.

October 1989
to February 1992;
Summer 1988

Baker & Botts
Dallas, Texas
Associate.

BAR ADMISSION:

State Bar of Texas, 1989.

REFERENCES AVAILABLE UPON REQUEST

SUZANNE C. MILLER
521 West Poinsettia Street
Culver City, California   90063
(310)   521-4949

PROFESSIONAL EXPERIENCE:

CORPORATE SECURITIES PRACTICE. Includes public offerings of debt and equity securities; public and private real estate syndications; mergers and acquisitions, including two major acquisitions as buyer's counsel; 1933 Act and 1934 Act compliance work, including regular and periodic reporting requirements, insider trading and short-swing profits rules, proxy solicitations for regular and special meetings of shareholders and sales of restricted securities under Rule 144; and general corporate work, including incorporations, liquidations, reincorporation mergers, drafting antitakeover provisions for charter documents, as well as drafting bylaws, corporate resolutions, and minutes.

EDUCATION:

University of California, Los Angeles School of Law
Los Angeles, California
J.D. 1988
Order of the Coif
Honors: Two American Jurisprudence Awards

University of California, at Los Angeles
Los Angeles, California
B.A. *summa cum laude*, Economics, 1985

EMPLOYMENT:

October 1988
to Present

Skadden, Arps, Slate, Meagher & Flom
Los Angeles, California
Associate.

Summer 1987

Sheppard, Mullin, Richter & Hampton
Los Angeles, California
Summer Associate. No offer extended.

BAR ADMISSION:

State Bar of California, 1988.

REFERENCES AVAILABLE UPON REQUEST

CHARLES ZIMMER
1602 Monroe Street
Chicago, Illinois 60603
(312) 212-3460

EDUCATION: **University of Chicago Law School**
Chicago, Illinois
J.D. 1987
Class Rank: Top 15%

University of Oregon
Eugene, Oregon
B.A. *cum laude*, Political Science, 1984
Phi Beta Kappa

EMPLOYMENT:

October 1987
to Present

Chapman & Cutler
Chicago, Illinois
Corporate Securities Associate. Involves broad range of experience in mergers and acquisitions, restructurings, financings, proxy contests, takeover defenses, variety of securities law and general corporate matters including employment agreements, shareholder agreements, corporate resolutions, loan documents, partnership agreements, and Delaware corporate law issues. Substantial experience with the Investment Advisors Act of 1940.

BAR ADMISSION: State Bar of Illinois, 1987.

LANGUAGE: Fluent in Korean.

PERSONAL INTERESTS: Basketball and swimming.

REFERENCES AVAILABLE UPON REQUEST

JAMES P. WILSON
1231 16th Street
Denver, Colorado   80202
(303)   823-4545

**PROFESSIONAL
EXPERIENCE:**

CORPORATE TAX/ OIL & GAS PRACTICE. Experience in structuring and implementing major oil and gas partnership exchange offers effected in compliance with Code Section 351, as well as exchange offer contemplating the consolidation of partnership interests into a "superpartnership." Responsibilities include participation in structuring transactions, drafting of tax and certain nontax portions of registration statements relating to exchange offers, negotiation of tax opinions, and preparation and review of requests for Federal tax rulings. Develop structure, tax documentation and opinions for syndicated offering of oil and gas limited partnership interests, both one- and two-tier. Review and supervise review of oil and gas syndicated offerings as due diligence counsel.

EMPLOYMENT:

December 1990
to Present

Sherman & Howard
Denver, Colorado
Tax Associate.

November 1989
to November 1990;
Summer 1988

Barenbaum & Weinshienk, P.C.
Denver, Colorado
Tax Associate.

EDUCATION:

University of Denver College of Law
Denver, Colorado
J.D. 1989
Class Rank: Top 20%
Member, University of Denver Law Journal

University of Nebraska
Lincoln, Nebraska
B.A. *magna cum laude*, Geography, 1986

BAR ADMISSION:

State Bar of Colorado, 1990.

PERSONAL INTERESTS: Racquetball and piano.

REFERENCES AVAILABLE UPON REQUEST

CARY GREEN
2214 West Abrams
Austin, Texas   75201
(512)   478-6212

PROFESSIONAL EXPERIENCE:	CORPORATE/VENTURE CAPITAL PRACTICE. Responsible for venture capital financings, mergers and acquisitions, licensing transactions, and related matters involving high technology and other companies. Handle general corporate and securities matters for privately held and publicly held corporations and venture capital firms, in industries including computer software, biotechnology, telecommunications, and energy.

EDUCATION:

University of Texas at Austin School of Law
Austin, Texas
J.D. 1990
Class Rank: Top 15%

Stanford   University
Palo Alto, California
B.A. *summa cum laude*, Political Science, 1987

EMPLOYMENT:

May 1992
to Present

Akin, Gump, Haver & Feld
Austin, Texas
Associate.

October 1990
to April 1992;
Summer 1989

Vinson & Elkins
Austin, Texas
Associate.

BAR ADMISSION: State Bar of Texas, 1990.

PERSONAL INTERESTS: Classical music, creative writing, and tennis.

REFERENCES AVAILABLE UPON REQUEST

SANDRA SULLIVAN
333 North Palm Drive, Apt. 205
Beverly Hills, California   90210
(310)   553-5656

EDUCATION:

Yale University Law School
New Haven, Connecticut
J.D. 1985
Class Rank: Approximately Top 20%
Note & Comment Editor, Yale Law Review

Catholic University
Washington, DC
B.S. with honors, Accounting, 1987
Honors/Activities: Honors Program Scholar; Beta Alpha Psi
(Accounting Honorary); Beta Gamma Sigma (Business Honorary);
Academic Excellence Scholarship.

EMPLOYMENT:

November 1992
to Present

Bird, Marella, Boxer, Wolpert & Matz
Los Angeles, California
Criminal (White Collar) Litigation Associate. Prepare motions
for summary judgment, motions in limine, judgment on the
pleadings and trial briefs. Prepare appellate motions to U.S.
Supreme Court and Ninth Circuit Court of Appeals. Prepare
memoranda of law and correspondence. Take and defend
depositions.

October 1987
to October 1992

U.S. Attorney's Office
Central District of California
Assistant U.S. Attorney.

November 1985
to September 1987;
Summer 1984

White & Case
Los Angeles, California
Litigation Associate.

BAR ADMISSION: State Bar of California, 1985.

PERSONAL INTERESTS: Tennis and sailing.

REFERENCES AVAILABLE UPON REQUEST

PAMELA A. ROSETTI
584 West Moore Drive, Apt. 32
Newark, New Jersey 07101
(201) 481-7390

**PROFESSIONAL
EXPERIENCE:**

EMPLOYEE BENEFITS PRACTICE. Responsible for plan and design of qualified and nonqualified retirement and health and welfare plans, including defined benefit and defined contribution plans, cash or deferred arrangements ("CODAs" or"401(k) plans"), employee stock ownership plans ("ESOPs"), cafeteria plans, voluntary employees' beneficiary associations ("VEBAs"), stock option plans, and various other deferred compensation arrangements, including stock bonus plans and "rabbi" trust; advise regarding federal tax and pension law matters, including nondiscrimination requirements, prohibited transactions, Department of Labor pension plan fiduciary compliance, and single and multiemployer plan funding issues with respect to the Employee Retirement Income Security Act of 1974 ("ERISA") and the Multiemployer Pension Plan Amendments Act of 1980 ("MEPPAA"); advise on federal employment law issues, including continuation healthcare ("COBRA") coverage, wage and hour, EEOC, and DFEH claims and severance pay benefits.

EMPLOYMENT:

May 1990
to Present

The Mutual Benefit Life Insurance Company
Newark, New Jersey
Second Vice President and Counsel.

October 1985
to April 1990;
Summer 1984

Epstein, Becker & Green
Newark, New Jersey
Associate.

EDUCATION:

Fordham University School of Law
New York, New York
J.D. 1985
Class Rank: Top 25%
Member, Fordham Law Review

State University of New York, at Albany
Albany, New York
B.A. *cum laude*, Political Science, 1982
G.P.A.: 3.6/4.0

BAR ADMISSION: State Bar of New Jersey, 1985.

LANGUAGE: Fluent in Italian.

PERSONAL INTERESTS: Italian cooking and opera.

REFERENCES AVAILABLE UPON REQUEST

DALE G. WYATT
11640 Kiowa Avenue, Apt. 311
Los Angeles, California 90049
(310) 474-3567

PROFESSIONAL EXPERIENCE:

EMPLOYEE BENEFITS PRACTICE. Responsible for plan and design of qualified and nonqualified retirement and health and welfare plans, including defined benefit and defined contribution plans, cash or deferred arrangements ("CODAs" or"401(k) plans"), employee stock ownership plans ("ESOPs"), cafeteria plans, voluntary employees' beneficiary associations ("VEBAs"), stock option plans, and various other deferred compensation arrangements, including stock bonus plans and "rabbi" trust; advise clients on federal tax and pension law issues, including nondiscrimination requirements, prohibited transactions, Department of Labor pension plan fiduciary compliance, and single and multiemployer plan funding issues with respect to the Employee Retirement Income Security Act of 1974 ("ERISA") and the Multiemployer Pension Plan Amendments Act of 1980 ("MEPPAA"); advise clients on California and federal employment law issues, including continuation healthcare ("COBRA") coverage, wage and hour, EEOC, and DFEH claims and severance pay benefits; employee manuals on personnel policies and procedures.

EDUCATION:

Vanderbilt University School of Law
Nashville, Tennessee
J.D. 1988
Class Rank: Top 15%
Member, Vanderbilt Law Review
Honors: Member, Moot Court Honors Program.

University of Tennessee
Knoxville, Tennessee
B.A. *summa cum laude*, English, 1985

EMPLOYMENT:

November 1990 to Present

Loeb & Loeb
Los Angeles, California
Associate.

October 1988 to October 1990

Baker & McKenzie
Los Angeles, California
Associate.

Summer 1987

Pension Benefit Guaranty Corporation
Washington, DC
Law Clerk.

PUBLICATIONS:	"An Analysis of Due Diligence in Employee Benefits," *Ohio Law Review,* Vol. 32, No. 4, Spring 1992.
	"A Review of Corporate Pension Plans--Are They Safe Havens?" *U.C.L.A. Law Review,* Vol. 19, No. 2, Fall 1991.
BAR ADMISSION:	State Bar of California, 1989.
LANGUAGE:	Fluent in Mandarin Chinese.
PERSONAL INTERESTS:	Tennis.

REFERENCES AVAILABLE UPON REQUEST

MARCY FEIGENBAUM
1801 Ranchito Drive
North Hollywood, California 91601
(818) 750-1620

PROFESSIONAL EXPERIENCE:	ENTERTAINMENT LITIGATION. Research and draft motions, pleadings and memoranda of law. Litigate matters of unfair competition, antitrust and infringement. Draft and negotiate artists' and producers' agreements. Take and defend depositions. Conduct client interviews.

EMPLOYMENT:

September 1992 to Present	**Armstrong & Hirsch** Los Angeles, California Entertainment Associate.
Summer 1991	**Irell & Manella** Los Angeles, California Summer Associate. Offer extended.
Summer 1990	**The Walt Disney Company** Burbank, California Intern.

EDUCATION:	**Stanford University Law School** Palo Alto, California J.D. 1992 Class Rank: #3 in the class Editor, Stanford Law Review
	Harvard University Cambridge, Massachusetts B.A. *summa cum laude*, Political Science, 1989

BAR ADMISSION:	State Bar of California, 1992.

PERSONAL INTERESTS:	Tennis and racquetball.

REFERENCES AVAILABLE UPON REQUEST

BENJAMIN ZAKOWSKI
726 Venice Boulevard
Venice, California   90034
(310)   746-3567

EDUCATION:

University of Minnesota Law School
Minneapolis, Minnesota
J.D. 1990
Class Rank: #10 in the class
Note & Comment Editor, Minnesota Law Review

University of California, at Los Angeles
Los Angeles, California
B.A. *summa cum laude*, Political Science, 1987
G.P.A.: 4.0/4.0

EMPLOYMENT:

September 1990
to Present;
Summer 1989

Loeb & Loeb
Los Angeles, California
Entertainment Litigation Associate. Represent directors, writers, actors, producers, and distributors in contract disputes. Draft motions, pleadings and memoranda of law. Take and defend depositions. Draft and negotiate settlement agreements.

Summer 1988

Orion Pictures
Los Angeles, California
Intern.

BAR ADMISSION: State Bar of California, 1990.

PERSONAL INTERESTS: Foreign films.

REFERENCES AVAILABLE UPON REQUEST

GAYLE ROUNDTREE
13792 Benedict Canyon
Beverly Hills, California   90210
(310)   275-6498

PROFESSIONAL EXPERIENCE:	ENTERTAINMENT TRANSACTIONAL PRACTICE. Draft and negotiate agreements and structure deals relating to production, financing, distribution, and licensing in all areas of entertainment practice, including theatrical motion pictures, television, basis and pay cable, videocassette, video disc, radio, and publishing. Represent performers, production companies, writers, stand-up comics, authors, and playwrights.

EDUCATION:

New York University School of Law
New York, New York
J.D. 1987
Class Rank: Top 12%
Editor, New York University Law Review

University of Chicago
Chicago, Illinois
B.A. *summa cum laude*, Political Science, 1984

EMPLOYMENT:

January 1992   **Bloom, Dekom & Hergott**
to Present   Los Angeles, California
                              Associate.

March 1990   **Mitchell, Silberberg & Knupp**
to December 1991   Los Angeles, California
                              Associate.

December 1988   **Manatt, Phelps & Phillips**
to February 1990   Los Angeles, California
                              Associate.

September 1987   **O'Melveny & Myers**
to November 1988;   Los Angeles, California
Summer 1986   Associate.

BAR ADMISSION: State Bar of California, 1987.

PERSONAL INTERESTS: Water skiing and sailing.

REFERENCES AVAILABLE UPON REQUEST

STACY ELIZABETH STANFORD
1402 Barrington Avenue, Apt. 306
Los Angeles, California   90049
(310)   474-2398

EMPLOYMENT:

January 1992 to Present	**Paramount Pictures Corporation** Los Angeles, California Vice President Business Affairs/Legal. Review and draft contracts and amendments to contracts with various artists. Assist in negotiation of contracts; research and analyze industry standards regarding employment matters.
November 1988 to December 1991; Summer 1987	**Rosenfeld, Meyer & Susman** Beverly Hills, California Entertainment Associate. Drafted and negotiated agreements and structured deals relating to production, financing, distribution, and licensing.

EDUCATION:

Emory University School of Law
Atlanta, Georgia
J.D. 1988
Class Rank: #4 in the class
Editor, Emory Law Journal

University of Arkansas
Fayetteville, Arkansas
B.A. *summa cum laude*, English, 1985

BAR ADMISSION:

State Bar of California, 1988.

PERSONAL INTERESTS:

Golf and racquetball.

REFERENCES AVAILABLE UPON REQUEST

HELENE COHEN
117 Washington Place
New York, New York   10005
(212)   710-1919

PROFESSIONAL EXPERIENCE:

ENVIRONMENTAL COMPLIANCE PRACTICE. Research and draft legal memoranda and motions in connection with CERCLA private party cost recovery litigation; conduct extensive research regarding CERCLA consent decree implementation issues and underground storage tank regulations; prepare seminar materials regarding the 1990 amendments to the enforcement, nonattainment, and mobile sources provisions of the Clean Air Act; counsel clients regarding various issues arising under federal and state hazardous waste regulations and water quality issues.

EDUCATION:

Columbia University School of Law
New York, New York
J.D. 1989
G.P.A.: 84.6

Brown   University
Providence, Rhode Island
B.A. *magna cum laude*, Political Science, 1986

EMPLOYMENT:

January 1992
to Present

Cadwalader, Wickersham & Taft
New York, New York
Associate.

November 1989
to December 1991;
Summer 1988

Beveridge & Diamond
New York, New York
Associate.

Summer 1988
(Split Summer)

Kaye, Scholer, Fierman, Hays & Handler
New York, New York
Summer Associate.

BAR ADMISSIONS: State Bars of New York, 1989; New Jersey, 1991.

PERSONAL INTERESTS: Foreign films, ballet, and French literature.

LANGUAGE: Fluency in French.

REFERENCES AVAILABLE UPON REQUEST

DANIEL ELLIOTT
1500 Figueroa Street, Apt. 101
Los Angeles, California 90004
(213)   865-7559

EDUCATION:	**University of Chicago Law School** Chicago, Illinois J.D. 1982 Class Rank: Top 18% **Loyola University** Chicago, Illinois B.A. *summa cum laude*, English, 1979 G.P.A.: 4.0/4.0

EMPLOYMENT:

March 1989 to Present	**Atlantic Richfield Company, Inc.** Los Angeles, California Environmental Attorney. Responsible for ensuring environmental compliance for all Western Division operations (California, Hawaii, Oregon, Washington, Nevada, Arizona, and Alaska). Duties include representing ARCO's upstream, downstream, and cogeneration operations in adminstrative and legislative proceedings, oil industry activities (WSPA), oil spill response Co-ops (Clean Seas, Clean Coastal Waters), and supervising outside counsel in lawsuits. Familiar with broad spectrum of state and federal environmental laws and regulations. Expertise in Superfund, pollution, insurance, air and water permitting, oil spills, administrative negotiation, and regulatory processes.
February 1986 to February 1989	**O'Melveny & Myers** Los Angeles, California Environmental Associate. Advised and represented clients with respect to civil and criminal federal and state environmental laws and regulations. Extensive administrative work and litigation involving the Clean Air Act, Clean Water Act and RCRA; significant Superfund litigation responsibility.
November 1982 to January 1986; Summer 1981	**Sonnenschein, Nath & Rosenthal** Chicago, Illinois Environmental Associate.
BAR ADMISSIONS:	State Bars of Illinois, 1982; California, 1986.
PERSONAL INTERESTS:	Golf, stamp collecting, and South American travel.
LANGUAGE:	Fluency in Spanish.

REFERENCES AVAILABLE UPON REQUEST

RITA B. HOFFMAN
1804 Spaulding Avenue
Los Angeles, California 90068
(213) 666-3212

EDUCATION:

Stanford University Law School
Palo Alto, California
J.D. 1991
Class Rank: Top 15%

University of Colorado
Boulder, Colorado
B.A. *summa cum laude*, Sociology, 1988

EMPLOYMENT:

November 1991
to Present

Cox, Castle & Nicholson
Los Angeles, California
Environmental Associate. Draft environmental indemnities and
related provisions for real estate contracts. Analyze complex
environmental problems in groundwater and soil. Negotiate
consent decrees, orders, and other government documents with
federal and state environmental officials. Monitor and advise
clients with respect to a major Superfund site and a state
Superfund site in the Silicon Valley.

Summer 1990

Kaye, Scholer, Fierman, Hays & Handler
Los Angeles, California
Summer Associate. No offer extended.

BAR ADMISSION: State Bar of California, 1992.

PERSONAL INTERESTS: Creative writing, travel, and photography.

REFERENCES AVAILABLE UPON REQUEST

DEBORAH LEE
1702 Orange Drive
Hollywood, California   90048
(213)   652-5412

EDUCATION:

University of California, Davis School of Law
Davis, California
J.D. 1990
Class Rank: Top 40%

Pepperdine University
Malibu, California
B.A. Political Science, 1987
G.P.A.: 3.6/4.0

EMPLOYMENT:

November 1990
to Present

Southern California Edison Company
Rosemead, California
Environmental Attorney. Practice includes water quality, water rights, licensing of hydroelectric facilities, hazardous substance communication, natural resources, and related issues.

Summer 1989

Environmental Protection Agency
San Francisco, California
Environmental Intern.

Summer 1988

Law Offices of Gregory D. Thatch
Sacramento, California
Summer Associate.

BAR ADMISSION: State Bar of California, 1990.

PERSONAL INTERESTS: Cooking, impressionist art, and modern dance.

REFERENCES AVAILABLE UPON REQUEST

JAMES J. REED
1301 18th Street NW
Washington, DC 20036
(202) 549-1515

EDUCATION:

Georgetown University Law Center
Washington, DC
J.D. 1986
Class Rank: Top 5%

Yale University
New Haven, Connecticut
B.A. Economics & Political Science, 1983
G.P.A.: 3.85/4.0

EMPLOYMENT:

October 1990
to Present

Hunton & Williams
Washington, DC
Of Counsel, Environmental Department. Provide litigation services and advice regarding environmental regulatory compliance and liability issues. Specific duties include advising national provider of health care regarding handling and disposal of medical/infectious waste pursuant to federal and state laws; advising seller of property containing underground storage tanks; and counseling chemical manufacturing company regarding compliance with federal and state requirements for hazardous waste remediation in settlement of an enforcement action.

July 1987
to August 1990

United States Environmental Protection Agency
Boston, Massachusetts
Assistant Regional Counsel, Superfund Section. Drafted and issued CERCLA Section 106 Orders; negotiated CERCLA Section 122(h) cost recovery settlements; negotiated site cleanup work plans; drafted and filed Superfund liens on property subject to response action under CERCLA; represented Agency in matters involving PRPs undergoing bankruptcy proceedings; assisted Department of Justice in litigating CERCLA cost recovery actions.

August 1986
to June 1987

Gibson, Dunn & Crutcher
Los Angeles, California
Litigation Associate.

Summer 1985

Sidley & Austin
Los Angeles, California
Summer Associate. No offer extended.

BAR ADMISSIONS:

State Bars of California, 1986; Massachusetts,1987; District of Columbia, 1990.

PERSONAL INTERESTS: Ice hockey and soccer.

REFERENCES AVAILABLE UPON REQUEST

ROBERT JAMES CACKLEBURN
1222 Eureka Place
Washington, D.C. 20036
(202)   908-7834

EDUCATION:	**Harvard University Law School** Cambridge, Massachusetts J.D. 1990 <u>Class Rank:</u> #3 in the class Editor in Chief, <u>Harvard Law Review</u> **Stanford University** Palo Alto, California B.A., *summa cum laude*, History, 1987 <u>G.P.A.:</u> 4.0/4.0

EMPLOYMENT:

Fall 1990 to Present; Summer 1989	**Arnold & Porter** Washington, DC <u>Environmental Litigation Associate.</u> Responsibilities include initiating and managing litigation involving recovery of remediation costs and negotiating agreements for remediation of petroleum contamination.
Summer 1988	**Environmental Protection Agency** Washington, DC <u>Intern</u>. Provided legal research assistance.

BAR ADMISSIONS: State Bars of Massachusetts, District of Columbia, 1990.

PERSONAL INTERESTS: Hiking and rock climbing.

LANGUAGES: Fluent in French, Spanish, Portugese, and German.

REFERENCES AVAILABLE UPON REQUEST

GRACE McCORMICK
786 Elmer Street
Trenton, New Jersey   08611
(609)   369-7967

EMPLOYMENT:

December 1990
to Present

Picco Mack Herbert Kennedy Jaffe & Yoskin
Trenton, New Jersey
Environmental Litigation Associate. Responsible for initiating
and managing environmental litigation involving recovery of
remediation costs and negotiating agreements for the remediation
of petroleum contamination.

September 1988
to November 1990

Adams, Duque & Hazeltine
New York, New York
Environmental Litigation Associate.

Summer 1987

Breed, Abbott & Morgan
New York, New York
Summer Associate. No offer extended.

EDUCATION:

Seton Hall University School of Law
Newark, New Jersey
J.D. 1988
Class Rank: Top 3%

University of Pittsburgh
Pittsburgh, Pennsylvania
B.A. *summa cum laude*, Art History, 1985
G.P.A.: 3.9/4.0
Phi Beta Kappa

BAR ADMISSIONS: State Bars of New York, 1988; New Jersey, 1990.

LANGUAGES: Fluent in French, Spanish, Portugese, and Italian.

PERSONAL INTERESTS: Renaissance art and European travel.

REFERENCES AVAILABLE UPON REQUEST

CYNTHIA PLATT
3490 Burbank Boulevard, Apt. 2
Burbank, California   91502
(818)   841-7231

PROFESSIONAL **EXPERIENCE:**	ENVIRONMENTAL LITIGATION PRACTICE. Research and draft motions, pleadings, and interrogatories. Argue motions in court. Take and defend depositions. Litigation involves recovery of remediation costs.

EMPLOYMENT:

November 1993 to Present; Summer 1992	**Latham & Watkins** Los Angeles, California Associate.
Summer 1991	**Honorable Joseph P. Sawtelle** Superior Court Appellate Department Los Angeles, California Extern.

EDUCATION:	**University of Southern California Law Center** Los Angeles, California J.D. 1993 Order of the Coif Editor in Chief, Southern California Law Review **University of Southern California** Los Angeles, California B.A. *summa cum laude*, 1990 G.P.A.: 4.0/4.0

BAR ADMISSION:	State Bar of California, 1993.

PERSONAL INTERESTS:	Board of Directors, Museum of Contemporary Art, Los Angeles; theatre and ballet.

REFERENCES AVAILABLE UPON REQUEST

JEFFREY DANIELS
513 State Street
Boston, Massachusetts 02109
(617) 523-5540

EDUCATION:

Vanderbilt University School of Law
Nashville, Tennessee
J.D. 1988
Class Standing: Top 13%

Dartmouth College
Hanover, New Hampshire
B.A. English, 1985
G.P.A.: 3.5/4.0

EMPLOYMENT:

August 1990
to Present

Goulston & Storrs
Boston, Massachusetts
Erisa and Employee Benefits Associate. Structure transactions to meet ERISA fiduciary standards; advise clients regarding fiduciary management of plans; structure procedures for clients' participation in fiduciary procedures. Structure and advise clients regarding the following retirement plans: defined benefit pension, profit-sharing, 401(k), and employee stock ownership plans (ESOPs).

September 1988
to July 1990;
Summer 1987

Hale & Dorr
Boston, Massachusetts
Corporate Associate.

BAR ADMISSION:

State Bar of Massachusetts, 1988.

PERSONAL INTERESTS:

Fishing, camping, and hiking.

REFERENCES AVAILABLE UPON REQUEST

STANTON LEACH
5786 Mammoth Avenue, Apt. 450
Denver, Colorado 80206
(303) 322-7897

PROFESSIONAL EXPERIENCE:

<u>ERISA AND EMPLOYEE BENEFITS PRACTICE.</u> Involved in all legal aspects of compensation, welfare benefit, and pension plans including DB, DC, 401(k), cafeteria, SERPSs, stock options, executive compensation, employee ownership, and incentives. Directly responsible for compliance with compensation and benefit plans with ERISA, I.R.S., Department of Labor, Security Exchange Commission, and other regulatory agency requirements. Draft plan documents and amendments and complete governmental reports including 5500s, 5310s, SARs, SPDs, and SEC filings.

EMPLOYMENT:

March 1989 to Present

Porter Memorial Hospital
Denver, Colorado
<u>Vice President, Compensation and Benefits Compliance.</u>

August 1988 to February 1989

Internal Revenue Service
Employee Plans/Exempt Organization Division
Trenton, New Jersey
<u>Tax Law Specialist.</u>

EDUCATION:

Seton Hall University School of Law
Newark, New Jersey
J.D. 1988
<u>Class Standing:</u> Top 15%

Colorado College
Colorado Springs, Colorado
B.A. Economics, 1985
<u>G.P.A.:</u> 3.5/4.0

BAR ADMISSIONS AND ORGANIZATIONS:

State Bars of New Jersey, 1988, Colorado, 1989. American Bar Association, Member, Section on Labor Law, American Compensation Association, Member.

PERSONAL INTERESTS: Rugby and soccer.

REFERENCES AVAILABLE UPON REQUEST

STEVEN QUAGMIRE
457 Sutter Street
San Francisco, California 94104
(415)   543-2785

EDUCATION:

Santa Clara University School of Law
Santa Clara, California
J.D. 1990
Class Rank: Top 20%

University of California, at Davis
Davis, California
B.A. *cum laude*, Political Science, 1987
G.P.A.: 3.6/4.0

EMPLOYMENT:

November 1990
to Present;
Summer 1989

Graham & James
San Francisco, California
ERISA Associate. Plan mergers, terminations, amendments, and administration; summary plan descriptions. Research areas include controlled group and affiliated service group analysis, ERISA preemption, COBRA, Social Security integration, Section 89 analysis, alienation provisions, QDRO determinations, participant loans, and vesting.

BAR ADMISSION: State Bar of California, 1990.

PERSONAL INTERESTS: Bicycling, sailing, and water skiing.

REFERENCES AVAILABLE UPON REQUEST

MARY RUSSELL
689 Fifth Avenue
New York, New York   10022
(212)   269-7209

PROFESSIONAL EXPERIENCE:	ERISA PRACTICE. Plan mergers, terminations, amendments, and administration; summary plan descriptions. Research areas include controlled group and affiliated service group analysis, ERISA preemption, COBRA, Social Security integration, Section 89 analysis, alienation provisions, QDRO determinations, participant loans, and vesting. Prior experience included general corporate, federal and state securities, and mergers and acquisitions.

EDUCATION:

Harvard University Law School
Cambridge, Massachusetts
J.D. 1985
Class Standing: Top 12%
Member, Harvard Law Review

University of California, Los Angeles
Los Angeles, California
B.A. *summa cum laude*, Political Science, 1982
Phi Beta Kappa

EMPLOYMENT:

November 1990
to Present
Cravath, Swaine & Moore
New York, New York
ERISA Associate.

November 1985
to October 1990;
Summer 1984
Curtis, Mallet-Prevost, Colt & Mosle
New York, New York
Corporate Associate.

BAR ADMISSION: State Bar of New York, 1985.

PERSONAL INTERESTS: Volunteer work: New York AIDS Hospice Center.

REFERENCES AVAILABLE UPON REQUEST

PETER ADAMS, III
34567 Corral Road
Dallas, Texas 75202
(214)   977-6120

EMPLOYMENT:

January 1988
to Present;
Summer 1987

Johnson & Gibbs
Dallas, Texas
Estate Planning & Probate Associate. Analysis and drafting
of estate plans, including charitable trusts; estate tax returns and
audits; decedent estates and postmortem trust administration; will
contests and probate litigation; speech writing and seminar outline
preparation. Analysis and drafting of wills, revocable trusts,
irrevocable trusts, charitable trusts, grantor retained income
trusts and generation skipping trusts; decedent estates, court-
supervised trusts, guardianship matters, and conservatorship
actions; preparation of estate and gift tax returns; representation
and negotiation of estate tax audits. Estate tax planning.

EDUCATION:

University of Texas at Austin School of Law
Austin, Texas
J.D. 1988
Class Standing: Top 12%
Member, Texas Law Review

Texas Tech University
Lubbock, Texas
B.S. *magna cum laude*, Engineering, 1985
G.P.A.: 3.85/4.0

BAR ADMISSION: State Bar of Texas, 1988.

PERSONAL INTERESTS: Rodeo and horseback riding.

REFERENCES AVAILABLE UPON REQUEST

KATHRYN SUTTON
1623 North 24th Street
Phoenix, Arizona 85004
(602) 252-3499

PROFESSIONAL EXPERIENCE:	<u>ESTATE PLANNING AND PROBATE PRACTICE.</u> Analysis and drafting of estate plans, including charitable trusts; estate tax returns and audits; decedent estates and postmortem trust administration; will contests and probate litigation; speech writing and seminar outline preparation. Analysis and drafting of wills, revocable trusts, irrevocable trusts, charitable trusts, grantor retained income trusts and generation skipping trusts; decedent estates, court-supervised trusts, guardianship matters, and conservatorship actions; preparation of estate and gift tax returns; representation and negotiation of estate tax audits. Estate tax planning.

EMPLOYMENT:

January 1989 to Present	**Brown & Bain** Phoenix, Arizona <u>Associate.</u>
October 1986 to December 1988; Summer 1985	**Shimmel, Hill, Bishop & Gruender** Phoenix, Arizona <u>Associate.</u>

EDUCATION:	**University of Arizona College of Law** Tucson, Arizona J.D. 1986 <u>Class Standing:</u> Top 10% **Arizona State University** Tempe, Arizona B.A. *magna cum laude*, English, 1983

BAR ADMISSION:	State Bar of Arizona, 1987.
PERSONAL INTERESTS:	Horseback riding, tennis, and southwestern cooking.

REFERENCES AVAILABLE UPON REQUEST

MARK R. BENTWORTH
7583 West Castle Road
Cheyenne, Wyoming 82001
(307) 638-0216

EMPLOYMENT:

September 1988
to Present

Rogers, Blythe & Lewis
Cheyenne, Wyoming
<u>Family Law Associate.</u> Practice includes all areas of family law including dissolution, annulment, custody, and support modification, as well as related area of adoption and guardianship. Appear at trial, OSC's, and hearings on various motions. Perform discovery. Negotiate and draft marital settlement agreements.

Summer 1987

Honorable Patricia Sandborn
Wyoming Supreme Court
<u>Extern.</u>

EDUCATION:

University of Wyoming College of Law
Laramie, Wyoming
J.D. 1988
<u>Class Rank:</u> Top 8%

University of Oklahoma
Norman, Oklahoma
B.A. *cum laude*, Sociology, 1985

BAR ADMISSION: State Bar of Wyoming, 1988.

PERSONAL INTERESTS: Photography.

REFERENCES AVAILABLE UPON REQUEST

JOAN CLARKE
1301 Riverwood Drive
Atlanta, Georgia 30328
(404) 395-0831

EDUCATION:

University of Georgia School of Law
Athens, Georgia
J.D. 1989
Class Rank: Top 20%

University of Tennessee
Nashville, Tennessee
B.A. *cum laude*, English, 1986

EMPLOYMENT:

September 1991
to Present

Bodker, Ramsey & Andrews
Atlanta, Georgia
Family Law Associate. Practice includes all areas of family law including dissolution, annulment, custody and support modification, as well as related area of adoption and guardianship. Appear at trial, OSC's, and hearings on various motions. Perform discovery. Negotiate and draft marital settlement agreements.

September 1989
to August 1991;
Summer 1988

Holt, Ney, Zatcoff & Wasserman
Atlanta, Georgia
General Corporate and Real Estate Associate. Drafted and revised various corporate and real estate documents, for formation, merger, and dissolution of Georgia and Delaware corporations and limited partnerships. Participated in document production for commercial loan transactions and acquisition agreements. Real estate practice included the drafting and revision of leases, mortgages, assignments, foreclosure documents, and sale and purchase agreements.

BAR ADMISSION: State Bar of Georgia, 1989.

PERSONAL INTERESTS: Song writing and piano.

REFERENCES AVAILABLE UPON REQUEST

COLLEEN COOPER
888 Pennsylvania Avenue
Washington, DC 20007
(202)   530-8241

EDUCATION:

American University, Washington College of Law
Washington, DC
J.D. 1990
Order of the Coif
Class Standing: Top 5%

Washington & Lee University
Lexington, Virginia
B.S. *magna cum laude*, Business Administration, 1987

EMPLOYMENT:

August 1990
to Present

Foley & Lardner
Washington, DC
Corporate Associate. Wide-ranging corporate practice including involvement in venture capital deals, stock offerings, and three public offerings. Negotiate the sale of a newspaper business, draft partnership agreements, joint venture agreements, stock purchase agreements, and shareholders' agreements. Formation of corporations and drafting of all corporate documents including certificates of determination.

Summer 1989

Covington & Burling
Washington, DC
Summer Associate. Offer extended.

BAR ADMISSIONS: State Bars of Maryland, 1990; District of Columbia, 1991.

PERSONAL INTERESTS: Foreign politics, theater, and travel.

REFERENCES AVAILABLE UPON REQUEST

SAMUEL KLINE
1565 North Ford Drive
Los Angeles, California 90035
(310)   255-4624

EDUCATION:
Northwestern University School of Law
Chicago, Illinois
J.D. 1985
Class Standing: Top 13%

University of Florida
Gainesville, Florida
B.A. *magna cum laude*, Political Science, 1982

EMPLOYMENT:

August 1990
to Present

Tuohy Foundation
Los Angeles, California
First Vice President. Corporate experience includes preparation and/or review of all proxy material, including annual meeting and other types of transactions, supervision of all aspects of corporate legal department, advising management of proposed corporate transactions, and supervision of all litigation and risk management. Representation of real estate subsidiary of parent corporation syndicator in acquisition and disposition of all types of real estate, representation of management corporation subsidiary in all types of leasing matters, supervision of outside counsel in litigation, bankruptcy, and financing areas.

September 1985
to July 1990;
Summer 1984

Allen, Matkins, Leck, Gamble & Mallory
Los Angeles, California
Corporate/Real Estate Associate. Representation of lenders in secured transactions, including negotiation and documentation of loans; representation of both purchasers and sellers of real estate and other assets, involving preparation of documentation and review of title, tenant leases, and zoning matters; and representation of real estate developers in various development projects.

BAR ADMISSION:
State Bar of California, 1985.

PERSONAL INTERESTS:
Water color painting, skiing, and hiking.

REFERENCES AVAILABLE UPON REQUEST

SALLY QUINN
34 Paradise Lane
Honolulu, Hawaii 96815
(808) 524-7623

EMPLOYMENT:

January 1991
to Present

Waikiki International Development Corp.
Honolulu, Hawaii
Assistant Corporate Counsel. Responsible for domestic and international advice and service to senior management, draft legal documentation and conduct negotiations with respect to new business start-ups; purchase, sale, or lease of assets; service agreements; acquisitions and divestitures; licensing agreements; and joint ventures. Supervise outside counsel.

September 1986
to December 1990;
Summer 1985

McCorriston Miho & Miller
Honolulu, Hawaii
Corporate Associate.

EDUCATION:

University Hawaii-Manoa
William S. Richardson School of Law
Honolulu, Hawaii
J.D. 1986
Class Standing: Top 18%
Member, University of Hawaii Law Review

Baylor University
Waco, Texas
B.A. *cum laude*, History, 1983

BAR ADMISSION:

State Bar of Hawaii, 1986.

PERSONAL INTERESTS:

Windsurfing and sailing.

REFERENCES AVAILABLE UPON REQUEST

MORGAN RAMSEY
1721 Main Street
Santa Monica, California 90274
(310) 555-2772

EDUCATION:

Northwestern University School of Law
Chicago, Illinois
J.D. 1993
Class Rank: Top 13%
Note and Comment Editor, Northwestern University Law Review

Alabama State University
Montgomery, Alabama
B.A. *magna cum laude*, Political Science, 1990
Activities: President, Black Student Association

EMPLOYMENT:

September 1993
to Present

Latham & Watkins
Los Angeles, California
Corporate Associate. Broad range of transactional experience
including secured lending, bankruptcy workouts, public finance,
general corporate issues, bank regulations, and securities
regulation.

Summer 1992

Gibson, Dunn & Crutcher
Los Angeles, California
Summer Associate. No offer extended.

BAR ADMISSION:

State Bar of California, 1993.

PERSONAL INTERESTS:

Basketball and football.

REFERENCES AVAILABLE UPON REQUEST

LAWRENCE G. FOX
612 10th Street, Apt. 301
Santa Monica, California   90405
(310)   826-3489

EMPLOYMENT:

October 1986
to Present;
Summer 1985

McKenna & Cuneo (Formerly McKenna, Conner & Cuneo)
Los Angeles, California
Government Contracts Associate. Involves extensive litigation before federal district and circuit courts, United States Claims Court, Court of Appeals for Federal Circuit, arbitration panels, state courts, and all major boards of contract appeals. Includes representation of major defense and aerospace contractors in contract disputes with United States; injunctive actions in Claims court and federal district courts; challenges to suspensions and debarments of government contractors and grantees; and product liability and Federal Tort Claims Act litigation growing out of performance of government contracts. Representation includes government prime contractors or subcontractors in disputes arising out of subcontracts. Such litigation involves standard commercial issues, generally is governed by U.C.C., and occurs before federal or state courts. Counsel clients regarding drafting, negotiation, and performance of government and commercial contracts; rights of parties under contract clauses and government regulations and preparation and submission of claims.

EDUCATION:

University of Pittsburgh School of Law
Pittsburgh, Pennsylvania
J.D. 1986
Class Rank: #3 in the class
Note & Comment Editor, University of Pittsburgh Law Review

University of California, at Irvine
Irvine, California
B.A. *magna cum laude,* History, 1983
G.P.A.: 3.8/4.0

BAR ADMISSION
& ACTIVITIES:

State Bar of California, 1987; Member, Federal & American Bar Association (Member, Public Contract Law Section).

PERSONAL INTERESTS: Sailing, reading historical novels, and electric guitar.

REFERENCES AVAILABLE UPON REQUEST

ADELINA MONROE
8761 East Oakdale Way
Detroit, Michigan 48226
(313)   961-2278

EDUCATION:

University of Detroit, Mercy School of Law
Detroit, Michigan
J.D. 1987
Class Rank: Top 5%
Note & Comment Editor, The Law Review

Wayne State University
Detroit, Michigan
B.A., Political Science, 1984
G.P.A.: 3.5/4.0

EMPLOYMENT:

August 1991
to Present

Michigan Health Care Corporation
Detroit, Michigan
Assistant Corporate Counsel. Provide advice on federal and state
regulation of all aspects of provision of medical services,
including formation, sale, merger and dissolution of medical
groups. Represent health care entity with respect to Department
of Health and Human Services Investigation; medical staff issues;
negotiation of provider contracts between hospitals, doctors,
medical groups and other health care entities. Provide general
advice on business and regulatory aspects of health care industry.
Interface with outside counsel.

September 1987
to July 1991;
Summer 1986

Riley and Roumell
Detroit, Michigan
Healthcare Associate.

BAR ADMISSION
& ACTIVITIES:

State Bar of Michigan, 1987; Vice President, American Black Bar
Association (1991-1992).

PERSONAL INTERESTS: Jogging, aerobics, and jazz dance.

REFERENCES AVAILABLE UPON REQUEST

LINDA SACKS
1804 Ridpath Drive
Los Angeles, California 90048
(213) 666-3313

PROFESSIONAL **EXPERIENCE:**	HEALTHCARE PRACTICE. Involves federal and state regulation of all aspects of provision of medical services, including formation, sale, merger, and dissolution of medical groups; advice on federal state anti-kickback and anti-referral laws and regulations; public offering of securities of medical equipment manufacturer; represent health care clients with respect to Department of Health and Human Services Investigations; medical staff issues; negotiation of provider contracts between hospitals, doctors, medical groups, and other health care entities; general advice on business and regulatory aspects of health care industry.

EDUCATION:

Temple University School of Law
Philadelphia, Pennsylvania
J.D. 1989
Class Rank: Top 15%
Member, Temple Law Review

University of California, San Diego
San Diego, California
B.S. *magna cum laude*, Public Health/Economics, 1986
G.P.A.: 3.9/4.0

EMPLOYMENT:

Fall 1989
to Present

Weissburg & Aronson
Los Angeles, California
Associate.

Summer 1988

Epstein, Becker & Green, P.C.
Los Angeles, California
Summer Associate. No offer extended.

BAR ADMISSION: State Bar of California, 1989.

PERSONAL INTERESTS: Active Board Member, American Cancer Society.

REFERENCES AVAILABLE UPON REQUEST

ARTHUR G. WARD
347 Boulder Lane
Wichita, Kansas 67201
(316) 681-2968

EMPLOYMENT:

March 1985
to Present

Health Care Plus of America, Inc.
Wichita, Kansas
Corporate Counsel. Provide advice on business and regulatory aspects of health care industry. Representing health care entity with respect to Department of Health and Human Services Investigation; medical staff issues; negotiation of provider contracts between hospitals, doctors, medical groups, and other health care entities.

September 1980
to February 1985;
Summer 1979

Entz, Anderson & Chanay
Topeka, Kansas
Healthcare Associate.

EDUCATION:

The University of Kansas School of Law
Lawrence, Kansas
J.D. 1980
Class Rank: Top 25%
Member, Kansas Law Review

Loyola University
Chicago, Illinois
B.A. *cum laude*, Political Science, 1977
G.P.A.: 3.6/4.0

BAR ADMISSION: State Bar of Kansas, 1980.

PERSONAL INTERESTS: Baseball.

REFERENCES AVAILABLE UPON REQUEST

RANDOLPH CASTILLO
13278 Grand Avenue, Apt. 275
Los Angeles, California 90017
(213)   623-4789

EMPLOYMENT:

October 1992
to Present

Barst & Mukamal
Los Angeles, California
<u>Immigration Associate.</u> Responsible for assisting foreign clients procure visas in connection with immigration of their key executives and employees. Process applications for visas and resolve difficulties arising from application process. Procure work permits, green cards for individual clients. Assist clients seeking political asylum.

Summer 1991

Immigration & Naturalization Service
Washington, DC
<u>Intern.</u>

EDUCATION:

Catholic University of America
Columbus School of Law
Washington, D.C.
J.D. 1992
<u>Class Rank:</u> Top 25%
Member, <u>The Catholic University of America Law Review</u>

West Virginia University
Morgantown, West Virginia
B.A. *cum laude,* Political Science, 1989
<u>G.P.A.:</u> 3.6/4.0

BAR ADMISSION
& ACTIVITIES:

State Bar of California, 1992; Member, American Immigration Lawyers Association.

LANGUAGES:

Fluent in Japanese, Spanish, French, and Farsi.

PERSONAL INTERESTS: Travelling, studying languages, and classical music.

REFERENCES AVAILABLE UPON REQUEST

SUSAN REID
143 Presidio
San Francisco, California 94105
(415) 453-1809

PROFESSIONAL EXPERIENCE:	<u>INSURANCE COVERAGE LITIGATION PRACTICE.</u> Experience in broad range of pretrial aspects of insurance coverage litigation. Authored approximately fifty coverage opinions on complex construction defect, environmental, investment loss, and intellectual property claims. Day-to-day management responsibility for several state and federal declaratory relief actions. Representation of primary carriers in several major construction defect actions against general contractor insureds. Representation of primary carriers in complex investment loss actions against corporate insureds and officers and directors. Representation of corporate insureds against carriers in declaratory relief actions.

EMPLOYMENT:

May 1990 to Present	**Cooper, White & Cooper** San Francisco, California <u>Associate.</u>
September 1988 to April 1990; Summer 1987	**Thelen, Marrin, Johnson & Bridges** San Francisco, California <u>Associate.</u>

EDUCATION:	**University of California, Hastings College of the Law** San Francisco, California J.D. 1988 <u>Class Rank:</u> Top 15% Editor, <u>Woman's Law Journal</u>
	Harvard University, Radcliffe College Cambridge, Massachusetts B.A. *cum laude*, English, 1985 <u>G.P.A.:</u> 3.68/4.0

BAR ADMISSION:	State Bar of California, 1988.

PERSONAL INTERESTS:	Bicycling.

REFERENCES AVAILABLE UPON REQUEST

JEFFREY A. SCHWARTZ
1672 Polk Street
San Francisco, California 94105
(415) 478-4890

PROFESSIONAL
EXPERIENCE:
INSURANCE BAD FAITH AND COVERAGE LITIGATION PRACTICE.
Extensive experience in all phases of pretrial litigation, second chair jury trials, and a court trial. Research and draft coverage opinions and reservation of rights letters, draft pleadings, demurrers, discovery motions, motions for summary judgment. Conduct and respond to all forms of discovery including depositions, prepare cases for trial, draft trial motions, briefs, motions in limine, jury instructions, prepare witnesses and exhibits for trial.

EDUCATION:
New York University School of Law
New York, New York
J.D. 1991
Class Rank: #12 in the class
Note & Comment Editor, New York University Law Review

Brown University
Providence, Rhode Island
B.A. *summa cum laude*, English, 1988

EMPLOYMENT:

March 1993
to Present
Buchalter, Nemer, Fields & Younger
San Francisco, California
Associate.

September 1991
to February 1993;
Summer 1990
LeBoeuf, Lamb, Leiby & Macrae
San Francisco, California
Associate.

BAR ADMISSION
& ACTIVITIES:
State Bar of California, 1991.
Member, Bar Association of San Francisco (Insurance Committee).

PERSONAL INTERESTS: Sailing and travel.

REFERENCES AVAILABLE UPON REQUEST

KURT FISCHL
9456 West Apple Street
Denver, Colorado 80002
(303) 751-7484

EMPLOYMENT:

July 1989 to Present	**Empire Casualty Company** Denver, Colorado Assistant General Counsel. Report to General Counsel. Consolidate claims files. Draft briefs and motions, research issues of law and draft memoranda, take and defend depositions, draft discovery responses. Interface with outside counsel.
September 1986 to June 1989	**Holmes & Starr** Denver, Colorado Insurance Defense Litigation Associate.
Summer 1985	**Montgomery & Andrews** Albuquerque, New Mexico Summer Associate. No offer extended.

EDUCATION:

University of New Mexico School of Law
Albuquerque, New Mexico
J.D. 1986
Class Rank: Top Third
Member, New Mexico Law Review

University of New Mexico
Albuquerque, New Mexico
B.A., English, 1983
G.P.A.: 3.5/4.0

BAR ADMISSION: State Bar of Colorado, 1986.

LANGUAGE: Fluent in Spanish.

PERSONAL INTERESTS: River rafting, hiking, and camping.

REFERENCES AVAILABLE UPON REQUEST

DANIEL TAKASUGI
456 Almaden Street
San Jose, California 95112
(408) 629-6666

EDUCATION:

Villanova University School of Law
Villanova, Pennsylvania
J.D. 1993
Class Rank: Top 40%

Pennsylvania State University
University Park, Pennsylvania
B.A., History, 1990
G.P.A.: 3.3/4.0

EMPLOYMENT:

Fall 1993
to Present;
Summer 1992

Campbell, Warburton, Britton, Fitzsimmons & Smith
San Jose, California
Insurance Defense Litigation Associate. Draft briefs and motions,
research issues of law and draft memoranda, take and defend
depositions, draft discovery responses.

Summer 1991

Honorable David Tatami
U.S. District Court for the Eastern District of Pennsylvania
Extern.

BAR ADMISSION: State Bar of California, 1993.

PERSONAL INTERESTS: Piano and baseball.

LANGUAGE: Fluent in Japanese.

REFERENCES AVAILABLE UPON REQUEST

ISAAC BLOOM
3459 42nd Street, Apt. No. 805
New York, New York   10022
(212)   980-5555

PROFESSIONAL
EXPERIENCE:

INTELLECTUAL PROPERTY LITIGATION PRACTICE. Research, write memoranda and draft pleadings on substantive and procedural issues in the areas of cable television, copyright, trademark, communications, broadcasting, FOIA, trade secrets, unfair competition, telephony, and general civil litigation. Take depositions and manage cases. Analyze cable programming contracts in connection with stock acquisitions. Perform syndicated exclusivity and network nonduplication studies of cable systems. Perform research on cable rate regulation and effective competition. Conduct cable due diligence studies and draft opinion letters for system refinancings. Perform research and draft pleadings on utility rate depreciation and incentive regulations. Prepare cases and witnesses, and conduct and defend cross-examinations in comparative broadcast proceedings.

EDUCATION:

New York University School of Law
New York, New York
J.D. 1987
Class Rank: Top 15%
Note & Comment Editor, New York University Law Review

St. John's University
Jamaica, New York
B.A. *summa cum laude*, History, 1984
G.P.A.: 4.0/4.0

EMPLOYMENT:

March 1990
to Present

Frankfurt, Garbus, Klein & Selz
New York, New York
Associate.

November 1987
to February 1990;
Summer 1986

Fish & Neave
New York, New York
Associate.

BAR ADMISSION:

State Bar of New York, 1987; American Intellectual Property Law Association; United States Trademark Association; American Law Institute.

PERSONAL INTERESTS: Racquetball, theater, and violin.

REFERENCES AVAILABLE UPON REQUEST

```
┌─────────────────────────────────────────────────────────┐
│          Intellectual Property Litigation Resume         │
└─────────────────────────────────────────────────────────┘
```

RAYMOND HERRERA
329 Sweetzer Avenue
West Hollywood, California   90069
(213)   752-1830

EDUCATION:

University of Washington School of Law
Seattle, Washington
J.D. 1989
<u>Class Rank:</u> Top 20%

University of Oregon
Eugene, Oregon
B.S. *summa cum laude*, Economics, 1986

EMPLOYMENT:

September 1989
to Present

Lyon & Lyon
Los Angeles, California
<u>Intellectual Property Litigation Associate.</u> Research, write memoranda and draft pleadings on substantive and procedural issues in the areas of cable television, copyright, trademark, communications, broadcasting, FOIA, trade secrets, unfair competition, telephony, and general civil litigation. Take depositions and manage cases. Analyze cable programming contracts in connection with stock acquisitions. Perform syndicated exclusivity and network nonduplication studies of cable systems. Perform research on cable rate regulation and effective competition. Conduct cable due diligence studies and draft opinion letters for system refinancings. Perform research and draft pleadings on utility rate depreciation and incentive regulations. Prepare cases and witnesses, and conduct and defend cross-examinations in comparative broadcast proceedings.

Summer 1988

Lane Powell Spears Lubersky
Seattle, Washington
<u>Summer Associate.</u> Offer extended.

BAR ADMISSION: State Bar of California, 1989.

PERSONAL INTERESTS: Off-road motorcycling.

REFERENCES AVAILABLE UPON REQUEST

GEORGE E. NEWBAUER
654 Dupont Circle Lane
Washington, DC 20036
(202)   955-3127

EDUCATION:

New York University School of Law
New York, New York
LL.M. *cum laude,* Taxation, 1990
G.P.A.: 3.6/4.0

University of Virginia School of Law
Charlottesville, Virginia
J.D. 1989
Class Rank: Top 4%
Editor, Virginia Tax Review

Vanderbilt University
Nashville, Tennessee
B.S. *summa cum laude*, Accounting, 1986
G.P.A.: 4.0/4.0

EMPLOYMENT:

November 1990
to Present

Howrey & Simon
Washington, DC
International Tax Associate. Experience includes U.S. inbound and outbound international structure planning for U.S. and foreign corporations; inbound real estate tax planning including FIRPTA; residency planning; Subpart F; foreign tax credit planning; tax treaties planning; international entity characterization; foreign national tax planning; and branch profits tax planning.

Summer 1988

McGuire, Woods, Battle & Boothe
Charlottesville, Virginia
Summer Associate. Offer Extended.

BAR ADMISSIONS: State Bars of Virginia, 1989; District of Columbia, 1990.

PERSONAL INTERESTS: Classical music.

REFERENCES AVAILABLE UPON REQUEST

JULIE BAKER
823 Flower Street
Los Angeles, California 90017
(213) 476-6204

PROFESSIONAL EXPERIENCE:

INTERNATIONAL TAX PRACTICE. Experience includes U.S. inbound and outbound international structure planning for U.S. and foreign corporations; international coproductions planning; inbound real estate tax planning including FIRPTA; residency planning; Subpart F; foreign tax credit planning; tax treaties planning; international entity characterization; foreign national tax planning; and branch profits tax planning.

EMPLOYMENT:

April 1991
to Present

Adams, Duque & Hazeltine
Los Angeles, California
Associate.

November 1989
to March 1991

Sidley & Austin
Los Angeles, California
Associate.

Summer 1987

Office of the Attorney General, Division of Civil Law-Business and Tax
Los Angeles, California
Law Clerk.

Summer 1986

United States Attorney's Office
Tax Division
Los Angeles, California
Law Clerk.

EDUCATION:

New York University School of Law
New York, New York
LL.M. *summa cum laude,* Taxation, 1989
G.P.A.: 3.9/4.0

Boston University School of Law
Boston, Massachusetts
J.D. 1988
Class Rank: Top 10%

Boston College
Chestnut Hill, Massachusetts
B.S. *cum laude,* Accounting, 1985

PUBLICATIONS: Co-Author; "International Taxation: Laws for the Informed," <u>International Tax Digest</u>, September 1992.

                            Co-Author; "Foreign Investments in the United States," <u>International Tax Journal</u>, January 1991.

BAR ADMISSION: State Bar of California, 1989.

PERSONAL INTERESTS: Trekking and photography.

REFERENCES AVAILABLE UPON REQUEST

Labor/Wrongful Termination Litigation Resume

JONATHAN G. BERRY
72 Cotton Road
Atlanta, Georgia 30303
(404) 525-3316

EDUCATION:

University of South Carolina School of Law
Columbia, South Carolina
J.D. 1989
Class Rank: Top 25%

University of Alabama
Birmingham, Alabama
B.A. *magna cum laude*, English, 1986
G.P.A.: 3.75/4.0

EMPLOYMENT:

August 1989
to Present;
Summer 1988

Jackson, Lewis, Schnitzler & Krupman
Atlanta, Georgia
Labor/ Wrongful Termination Litigation Associate. Manage and supervise junior attorneys in labor and employment cases, including race, sex, and national origin discrimination and wrongful termination matters. Draft pleadings and discovery, prepare legal motions, present oral arguments in state and federal courts. Take and defend depositions. Trial preparation for labor and employment law cases, primarily state and federal discrimination and wrongful termination matters. Conduct administrative hearings before Department of Employment Development; Unemployment Insurance Appeals Board; and Department of Industrial Relations, Division of Labor Standards Enforcement. Prepare and present witnesses in investigatory proceedings before the U.S. National Labor Relations Board and U.S. Equal Employment Opportunity Commission.

**BAR ADMISSION
& ACTIVITIES:**

State Bar of Georgia, 1989; Member, Atlanta and American (Member, Section on Labor and Employment Law) Bar Associations.

PERSONAL INTERESTS: Lawn bowling and golf.

REFERENCES AVAILABLE UPON REQUEST

FRANCIS GREENWICH
3468 West 18th Street, Apt. 506
Chicago, Illinois 60606
(312) 332-6142

PROFESSIONAL EXPERIENCE:

LABOR AND WRONGFUL TERMINATION LITIGATION PRACTICE.
Manage and supervise junior attorneys in labor and employment cases, including race, sex, and national origin discrimination and wrongful termination matters. Draft pleadings and discovery, prepare legal motions, present oral arguments in state and federal courts. Take and defend depositions. Trial preparation for labor and employment law cases, primarily state and federal discrimination and wrongful termination matters. Conduct administrative hearings before Department of Employment Development; Unemployment Insurance Appeals Board; and Department of Industrial Relations, Division of Labor Standards Enforcement. Prepare and present witnesses in investigatory proceedings before the U.S. National Labor Relations Board and U.S. Equal Employment Opportunity Commission.

EMPLOYMENT:

August 1992 to Present

Seyfarth, Shaw, Fairweather & Geraldson
Chicago, Illinois
Associate.

September 1990 to July 1992; Summer 1989

Oppenheimer Wolff & Donnelly
Chicago, Illinois
Associate.

EDUCATION:

De Paul University College of Law
Chicago, Illinois
J.D. 1990
Class Rank: Top 4%
Note & Comment Editor, De Paul Law Review

University of Illinois
Chicago, Illinois
B.A. *cum laude*, English, 1987

BAR ADMISSION:

State Bar of Illinois, 1990.

PERSONAL INTERESTS: Poetry.

REFERENCES AVAILABLE UPON REQUEST

BARBARA McANDREWS
4709 McKinley Drive
Burlington, Vermont 05406
(802) 862-7241

PROFESSIONAL EXPERIENCE:	LAND USE PRACTICE. Represent corporate clients in land use and zoning matters; document, perform title work, and draft loan documents; negotiate and draft real estate purchase and sale agreements and office, industrial, and retail leases; document loan transactions secured by real and personal property.

EMPLOYMENT:

January 1990 to Present	**Burak & Anderson** Burlington, Vermont Associate.
September 1988 to December 1989; Summer 1987	**Gravel & Shea** Burlington, Vermont Associate.

EDUCATION:	**Vermont Law School** South Royalton, Vermont J.D. 1988 Class Rank: Top 15% Member, Vermont Law Review
	Boston University Boston, Massachusetts B.A. *cum laude*, English, 1985 G.P.A.: 3.6/4.0

BAR ADMISSION:	State Bar of Vermont, 1988.

PERSONAL INTERESTS:	Hiking and water color painting.

REFERENCES AVAILABLE UPON REQUEST

WILLIAM RAMSEY
60 Elm Street
Long Beach, California   90808
(310)   982-3888

EDUCATION:	**University of California, at Berkeley**
	Boalt Hall
	Berkeley, California
	J.D. 1990
	G.P.A.: 84.1

Duke University
Durham, North Carolina
B.A. *summa cum laude*, History, 1987
G.P.A.: 4.0/4.0

EMPLOYMENT:

Fall 1990
to Present;
Summer 1989

Alschuler, Grossman & Pines
Los Angeles, California
Land Use Associate. Represent corporate clients in land use and zoning matters; document, perform title work, and draft loan documents for acquisition of oil and gas, lode and placer mining and geothermal properties; negotiate and draft real estate purchase and sale agreements and office, industrial, and retail leases; document loan transactions secured by real and personal property; perform general business transactional work.

PUBLICATIONS:

Co-Author; "Zoning Variances--Are They the Way Out," California Environmental Journal, August 1992.

Co-Author; "Land Use Issues in California," California Environmental Journal, March 1992.

BAR ADMISSION:

State Bar of California, 1990.

PERSONAL INTERESTS: Surfing, water skiing, and scuba diving.

REFERENCES AVAILABLE UPON REQUEST

CHARLES S. ROBBINS
568 East Caravelle Road
Fort Lauderdale, Florida   33301
(305)   525-7490

EMPLOYMENT:

November 1993
to Present;
Summer 1992

Greenspoon, Marder, Hirschfeld & Rafkin, P.A.
Fort Lauderdale, Florida
Land Use Associate. Represent corporate clients in land use and
zoning matters; document, perform title work, and draft loan
documents; negotiate and draft real estate purchase and sale
agreements and office, industrial, and retail leases; document loan
transactions secured by real and personal property.

EDUCATION:

University of Florida College of Law
Gainesville, Florida
J.D. 1993
Class Rank: Top 20%
Member, Florida Law Review

University of Georgia
Athens, Georgia
B.A. *magna cum laude*, English, 1990
G.P.A.: 3.75/4.0

BAR ADMISSION: State Bar of Florida, 1993.

PERSONAL INTERESTS: Windsurfing.

REFERENCES AVAILABLE UPON REQUEST

NANCY CANTOR
2106 Pine Street
Santa Monica, California 90403
(310) 285-7831

EDUCATION:

Santa Clara University School of Law
Santa Clara, California
J.D. 1978
Class Rank: Top 30%

Lewis & Clark College
Portland, Oregon
B.A. History, 1975
G.P.A.: 3.5/4.0

EMPLOYMENT:

September 1980
to Present

Greene, Broillet, Taylor & Wheeler
Santa Monica, California
Medical Malpractice Associate. Experience includes pharmaceutical and medical malpractice litigation. Extensive law and motion and discovery experience. Take and defend depositions of expert witnesses. Major responsibility in cases with liability exposure exceeding one million dollars.

September 1978
to August 1980;
Summer 1977

Law Offices of David M. Harney
Los Angeles, California
Medical Malpractice Associate.

BAR ADMISSION:

State Bar of California, 1978; Admitted to all U.S. District Courts in California; multidistrict litigation in Federal Courts.

PERSONAL INTERESTS: Sailing, snorkeling, and bicycling.

REFERENCES AVAILABLE UPON REQUEST

RANDALL WHITEWATER
23400 Burbank Boulevard, Apt. 308
Van Nuys, California 91411
(818) 785-7842

EDUCATION:

University of San Diego School of Law
San Diego, California
J.D. 1987
Class Rank: Top 40%

University of Hawaii
Honolulu, Hawaii
B.S. *cum laude*, Biology, 1975

**LEGAL
EMPLOYMENT:**

September 1987
to Present

Bonne, Bridges, Mueller, O'Keefe & Nichols
Los Angeles, California
Senior Associate. Responsible for management of all aspects of extensive medical malpractice case load, including law and motion, discovery, expert witness retention and reviews, legal research, liability analysis, and client contact.

**OTHER
EMPLOYMENT:**

June 1975 to
July 1984

University of Hawaii Hospital
Honolulu, Hawaii
Registered Nurse.

BAR ADMISSION:

State Bar of California, 1987; Admitted to practice in all districts of the Federal Court in the State of California.

PERSONAL INTERESTS: Scuba diving and surfing.

REFERENCES AVAILABLE UPON REQUEST

JOAN DEMING
1604 Church Street
New Haven, Connecticut   06511
(203)   473-6646

PROFESSIONAL EXPERIENCE:	<u>PATENT LAW.</u> Head legal department of twelve employees. Litigate all interparty cases in U.S. District and Appellate Courts, and Trademark Trial and Appeal Board. Negotiate and draft U.S. and International sales contracts, manufacturing agreements, licenses. Handle all Federal Trade Commission matters and all industrial property filings in the United States and other countries.
EDUCATION:	**Columbia University School of Law** New York, New York J.D./M.B.A. 1980 Order of the Coif Member, <u>Columbia Law Review</u> **Massachusetts Institute of Technology** Cambridge, Massachusetts B.S.E.E. 1977 <u>G.P.A.:</u> 3.9/4.0
EMPLOYMENT:	
March 1987 to Present	**Chesebrough-Pond's Inc.** Greenwich, Connecticut <u>Senior Attorney.</u>
August 1980 to February 1987; Summer 1979	**Bachman & LaPointe, P.C.** New Haven, Connecticut <u>Patent Associate.</u>
BAR ADMISSIONS & ACTIVITIES:	State Bar of Connecticut, 1980; Registered to practice before U.S. Patent and Trademark Office. Member, American Bar Association (Patent, Trademark and Copyright Law Section); Connecticut Patent Law Association; International Patent and Trademark Association.
PERSONAL INTERESTS:	Opera, ballet, and classical music.

REFERENCES AVAILABLE UPON REQUEST

RICHARD VOSS
8746 MacArthur Court
Newport Beach, California 92660
(714) 322-7964

EDUCATION:

Loyola Marymount University Law School
Los Angeles, California
J.D. 1987
Order of the Coif
Member, Loyola Law Review

University of California, at Los Angeles
Los Angeles, California
B.S.E.E. 1984
G.P.A.: 3.5/4.0

EMPLOYMENT:

January 1989
to Present

ATV Systems
Anaheim, California
Assistant Patent Counsel. Manage all activities of department with a $10 million annual budget; direct and supervise ten senior patent attorneys, one patent agent, and one patent draftsman. Duties include directing patent licensing activities, setting policies and procedures for the protection of intellectual property, overseeing the patent prosecution of staff, collecting and paying royalties, and handling patent and trade secret litigation. Matters include key electronic technologies of digital/videotape recording, data storage and retrieval systems, video image manipulation (special effects), data compression, error correction coding, error concealment, and magnetic tape production processes.

November 1987 to
December 1988;
Summer 1986

Lyon & Lyon
Los Angeles, California
Patent Associate. Prepared and assisted in preparation and prosecution of patent and trademark applications. Conducted validity, infringement, and right to use searches and studies.

**BAR ADMISSIONS
& ACTIVITIES:**

State Bar of California, 1987; U.S. Patent and Trademark Office, 1988; American Corporate Patent Counsel Association; American Intellectual Property Law Association; Orange County Patent and Trademark Law Association.

PERSONAL INTERESTS: Chess and airplane model building.

REFERENCES AVAILABLE UPON REQUEST

PAUL KRAUSE
438 Cactus Lane
Phoenix, Arizona   85014
(602)   264-1786

EMPLOYMENT:

January 1988 to Present	**Law Offices of Paul Krause** Phoenix, Arizona Personal Injury Litigation Practice. Responsible for wide range of personal injury insurance litigation matters, including coverage, vehicle, premises, and product liability cases. Handle all stages of litigation including drafting and editing of complaints, cross complaints, answers, demurrers, discovery matters, summary judgment motions; and arbitration and trial briefs. Take and defend depositions and depose expert witnesses. Have tried to conclusion jury trials in State and Federal Courts and numerous Arbitration and Court trials.
October 1985 to December 1987; Summer 1984	**Jennings, Kepner & Haug** Phoenix, Arizona Insurance Defense Litigation Associate.

EDUCATION:

University of Arizona College of Law
Tucson, Arizona
J.D. 1985
Class Rank: Top 40%

Arizona State University
Tempe, Arizona
B.A. English, 1982
G.P.A.: 3.4/4.0

BAR ADMISSION: State Bar of Arizona, 1985.

PERSONAL INTERESTS: Baseball.

REFERENCES AVAILABLE UPON REQUEST

JOSEPH MADDEN
2912 42nd Street, Apt. 382
New York, New York 10171
(212) 698-3514

PROFESSIONAL EXPERIENCE:

PERSONAL INJURY LITIGATION PRACTICE. Responsible for wide range of personal injury insurance litigation matters, including, coverage, vehicle, premises, and product liability cases. Handle all stages of litigation including drafting and editing of complaints, cross complaints, answers, demurrers, discovery matters, summary judgment motions; and arbitration and trial briefs. Take and defend depositions and depose expert witnesses. Have tried to conclusion jury trials in State and Federal Courts and numerous Arbitration and Court trials.

EMPLOYMENT:

January 1991
to Present

Bauman & Kunkis, P.C.
New York, New York
Associate.

October 1987
to December 1990;
Summer 1986

Butler, Fitzgerald & Potter
New York, New York
Associate.

EDUCATION:

New York Law School
New York, New York
J.D. 1987
Class Rank: Top Third

State University of New York, at Buffalo
Buffalo, New York
B.A. *cum laude*, Political Science, 1984

BAR ADMISSION:

State Bar of New York, 1987.
New York and U.S. District Court, Southern and Eastern Districts of New York.

PERSONAL INTERESTS: Theater, baseball, and writing mystery short stories.

REFERENCES AVAILABLE UPON REQUEST

BRUCE KINGMAN
1640 79th Street
Los Angeles, California   90048
(213)   398-7653

PROFESSIONAL **EXPERIENCE:**	PRODUCT LIABILITY LITIGATION PRACTICE. Involves primarily total case management of products liability cases. Includes all levels of responsibility from beginning to settlement/trial of each matter. Responsible for all phases of litigation, including discovery, taking and defending depositions, expert witness depositions. Have successfully tried twelve cases. Most recent case included settlement of a defective machine products liability case involving Dual Capacity doctrine.
EDUCATION:	**Southwestern University School of Law** Los Angeles, California J.D. 1985 Class Rank: Approximately Top 15% **San Diego State University** San Diego, California B.A. *cum laude*, English, 1982 G.P.A.: 3.6/4.0

EMPLOYMENT:

January 1991 to Present	**Law Offices of Bruce Kingman** Los Angeles, California Solo Practioner.
November 1985 to December 1990; Summer 1984	**Knapp, Peterson & Clarke** Glendale, California Products Liability Associate.

BAR ADMISSION:	State Bar of California, 1986.
PERSONAL INTERESTS:	Basketball and antique cars.

REFERENCES AVAILABLE UPON REQUEST

CYNTHIA PEREZ
2120 Montana Avenue
Santa Monica, California   90403
(310)   828-6789

EDUCATION:	**Indiana University/Bloomington School of Law** Bloomington, Indiana J.D. 1988 <u>Class Rank:</u> Top 20% Member, <u>Indiana Law Journal</u>
	Purdue University Lafayette, Indiana B.A. *cum laude*, Psychology, 1985

EMPLOYMENT:

November 1988 to Present; Summer 1987	**Carlsmith, Ball, Wichman, Murray, Case, Mukai & Ichiki** Los Angeles, California <u>Product Liability Associate.</u> Participate in all stages of discovery, law and motions practice, and arbitrations. Act as managing attorney of major automobile manufacturer's national repository for products liability litigation; responsibilities include coordination of document-related discovery nationwide, supervising other attorneys and paralegals, interacting with in-house counsel and outside counsel nationwide regarding discovery-related policies and protocols.
Summer 1986	**Honorable Maxwell Ingrow** Indiana Supreme Court Bloomington, Indiana <u>Extern.</u>

BAR ADMISSION:	State Bar of California, 1988.

PERSONAL INTERESTS:	Latin American literature.

REFERENCES AVAILABLE UPON REQUEST

KATHY FACTOR
200 Victoria Street
Boston, Massachusetts 02110
(617) 850-5575

EMPLOYMENT:

October 1990 to Present	**Bringham, Dana & Gould** Boston, Massachusetts <u>Real Estate Development Associate</u>. Represents clients in a broad range of real estate transactions, emphasizing real property transfers, leasing, commercial and residential real property development, land use regulation, and environmental law. Negotiate and prepare documentation of real property purchase and sale agreements; commmercial, industrial, and residential leases; financing agreements; easements; and listing agreements. Perform title review and other required due diligence. Advise buyers and sellers of contaminated or potentially contaminated property. Outline entitlement process for proposed developments. Clients include real estate developers, financial institutions, property owners and public agencies.
Summer 1989	**Hill & Barlow** Boston, Massachusetts <u>Summer Associate</u>. Offer extended.

EDUCATION:

Boston College Law School
Chestnut Hill, Massachusetts
J.D. 1990
<u>Class Rank:</u> Top Third
<u>Honors:</u> Dean's List 1989; American Jurisprudence Award in Real Property.

Boston College
Chestnut Hill, Massachusetts
B.S. Business Administration, 1987
Emphasis in Finance and Business Economics
<u>Honors:</u> Dean's List; School of Business Administration Award of Merit.

BAR ADMISSION: State Bar of Massachusetts, 1990.

PERSONAL INTERESTS: Tennis, skiing, and traveling.

REFERENCES AVAILABLE UPON REQUEST

FRANK GREENE
17 Calvert Street
Baltimore, Maryland 21202
(410) 385-6515

EDUCATION:

Georgetown University Law Center
Washington, DC
J.D. 1988
Class Rank: Top 3%
Editor, The Georgetown Law Journal

University of California, at Santa Barbara
Santa Barbara, California
B.A. *magna cum laude*, Philosophy, 1985

EMPLOYMENT:

November 1988
to Present;
Summer 1987

Miles & Stockbridge
Baltimore, Maryland
Real Estate Development Associate. General representation of real estate developers and investors in commercial, mixed use, and residential developments, including office buildings, industrial and warehousing facilities, shopping centers, hotels, and residential subdivisions. This representation includes the negotiation and documentation of all matters related to the acquisition and disposition of properties, space, and ground leases; construction and permanent financings; and the formation of partnerships and joint ventures; and also involves subdivision map work, governmental entitlement and regulatory work, supervision of real estate related litigation, and general corporate work.

BAR ADMISSION: State Bar of Maryland, 1988.

PERSONAL INTERESTS: Hiking and basketball.

REFERENCES AVAILABLE UPON REQUEST

GARY SIMON KORSHAK
376 North Rexford Drive
Beverly Hills, California 90210
(310) 276-4563

PROFESSIONAL EXPERIENCE:

REAL ESTATE DEVELOPMENT PRACTICE. Represent clients in broad range of real estate transactions, involving real property transfers, leasing, commercial and residential real property development, land use regulation and environmental law. Negotiate and prepare documentation of real property purchase and sale agreements; commmercial, industrial, and residential leases; financing agreements; easements; and listing agreements. Perform title review and other required due diligence. Advise buyers and sellers of contaminated or potentially contaminated property. Outline entitlement process for proposed developments. Clients include real estate developers, financial institutions, and property owners.

EMPLOYMENT:

May 1990 to Present

Freshman, Marantz, Orlanski, Cooper & Klein
Beverly Hills, California
Real Estate Associate.

September 1987 to April 1990

Allen, Matkins, Leck, Gamble & Mallory
Los Angeles, California
Real Estate Associate.

Summer 1986

Honorable George Peacock
Supreme Court of Delaware
Extern.

EDUCATION:

George Washington University
The National Law Center
Washington, DC
J.D. 1987
Class Rank: #6 in the class
Editor, George Washington Law Review

Washington & Lee University
Lexington, Virginia
B.A. Political Science, 1984
G.P.A.: 3.35/4.0

BAR ADMISSION: State Bar of California, 1987.

PERSONAL INTERESTS: Traveling and chess.

REFERENCES AVAILABLE UPON REQUEST

JAMES MIYAKO
329 Bay View Ave., Apt. 390
San Francisco, California 94104
(415) 677-4333

EMPLOYMENT:

September 1990
to Present;
Summer 1989

Morrison & Foerster
San Francisco, California
Real Estate Development Associate. Represent foreign investor
clients in broad range of real estate transactions. Assist in
acquisition and operation of commercial and residential
real estate. Advise foreign investors regarding tax laws and
regulation. Establish foreign based holding companies. Draft real
estate limited partnerships.

EDUCATION:

Duke University School of Law
Durham, North Carolina
J.D. 1990
Class Rank: Top 12%
Note & Comment Editor, Duke Law Journal

University of California, at Berkeley
Berkeley, California
B.A. *magna cum laude*, English, 1987
G.P.A.: 3.85/4.0

BAR ADMISSION: State Bar of California, 1990.

LANGUAGE: Fluent in Japanese.

PERSONAL INTERESTS: Tennis and bicycling.

REFERENCES AVAILABLE UPON REQUEST

TIMOTHY SCHULTZ
1602 Jefferson Street
Detroit, Michigan 48243
(313) 987-8389

EDUCATION:

University of Michigan Law School
Ann Arbor, Michigan
J.D. 1988
Class Rank: Top 17%

American Graduate School of International Management (Thunderbird)
Master of International Management, Awarded with Distinction
December 1979

Michigan State University
East Lansing, Michigan
B.A. *cum laude*, Political Science, 1977

EMPLOYMENT:

September 1988 to Present

Dykema Gossett
Detroit, Michigan
Real Estate Development Associate. Negotiate, draft, and review various real estate-related agreements, including purchase/sale contracts, commercial and residential leases, option agreements, limited partnership agreements, land use and zoning, real property financing and loan documentation, conveyances, real property exchanges, construction documents, and mechanics liens.

1980 to 1985

Comerica Bank - Detroit
Detroit, Michigan
Assistant Vice-President. Managed commercial construction loan portfolio in excess of $29 million. Drafted and negotiated original loan documents and agreements. Developed new prospects and enhance relations with existing clients.

Corporate Banking Officer. Managed staff of twelve professional and staff-level personnel. Designed applications for use of micro-computer in financial analysis. Trained professional level commercial credit analysts.

BAR ADMISSION: State Bar of Michigan, 1988.

REFERENCES AVAILABLE UPON REQUEST

Real Estate Development and Finance Resume

TANYA RAPPAPORT
193 Manhole Avenue, Apt. 4
San Francisco, CA 94104
(415) 422-6789

EMPLOYMENT:

November 1988
to Present;
Summer 1987

Landels, Ripley & Diamond
San Francisco, California
Real Estate Development and Finance Associate. Extensive experience in structuring, documenting, and negotiating real estate related transactions, with emphasis in: acquisitions (both asset and partnership) of industrial, office, retail, resort hotel, and residential (apartment) properties (transactions ranging in size from $9 million to over $8 million), including I.R.C. Section 1031 tax-deferred exchanges; financings and loan workouts (transactions ranging in size from $200,000 to over $3 million); industrial, office, and retail space leasing; ground leases; and master leases. Extensive experience in managing real estate transactions from preliminary negotiations to closing, including drafting letters of intent and transaction documentation (sale and partnership agreements, loan documents, leases), reviewing title and negotiating title insurance coverage, coordinating special counsel, and organizing and managing closings.

Summer 1986

Assemblyman William J. Filante, 9th District
State Capitol, Sacramento, California
Legislative Intern. Conducted research and assisted with office administration.

EDUCATION:

University of California, Hastings College of Law
San Francisco, California
J.D. 1988
Class Rank: Approximately Top 40%

University of California, Graduate School of Business Administration
Berkeley, California
M.B.A. 1988

Stanford University
Palo Alto, California
B.A. Political Science with Honors, 1985

BAR ADMISSION: State Bar of California, 1988.

PERSONAL INTERESTS: Traveling, sailing, classical music.

REFERENCES AVAILABLE UPON REQUEST

SUSAN CHAN
345 Seaport Lane
Seattle, Washington   98101
(206)   622-7135

PROFESSIONAL **EXPERIENCE:**	<u>REAL ESTATE FINANCE PRACTICE.</u> Real estate financing transactions, including construction financing, refinancings, municipal finance, revolving facilities, securitizing real estate collateral in multistate asset based transactions, leveraged buyouts, loan restructuring, loan workouts, deeds in lieu of foreclosure, nonjudicial foreclosures.
EDUCATION:	**University of Washington School of Law** Seattle, Washington J.D. 1988 <u>Class Rank:</u> #1 in the class Editor in Chief, <u>Washington Law Review</u>
	Reed College Portland, Oregon B.A. *magna cum laude*, English, 1985 <u>G.P.A.:</u> 3.8/4.0

EMPLOYMENT:

July 1993 to Present	**Perkins Coie** Seattle, Washington <u>Associate.</u>
November 1988 to June 1993; Summer 1987	**Davis Wright & Tremaine** Seattle, Washington <u>Associate.</u>

BAR ADMISSION:	State Bar of Washington, 1988.
PERSONAL INTERESTS:	Photography.

REFERENCES AVAILABLE UPON REQUEST

DAVID EISEN
1601 Pearl Avenue
Louisville, Kentucky   40202
(502)   598-7568

EDUCATION:

Stanford University Law School
Palo Alto, California
J.D. 1991
Class Rank: Top 20%

University of Kentucky
Lexington, Kentucky
B.A. *cum laude*, History, 1988

EMPLOYMENT:

October 1991
to Present

Brown, Todd & Heyburn
Louisville, Kentucky
Real Estate Finance Associate. Represent institutional lenders, developers, and other clients. Document and negotiate a variety of transactions including construction and permanent loan financing; loan financing involving multistate real property security and loan workouts; and formation of partnerships and real property acquisition.

Summer 1990

Brown & Bain
Palo Alto, California
Summer Associate. Offer extended.

BAR ADMISSION: State Bar of Kentucky, 1991.

PERSONAL INTERESTS: Horseback riding, and show dog breeding.

REFERENCES AVAILABLE UPON REQUEST

HARRY GOLDMAN
80 South Ninth Street
Minneapolis, Minnesota 55402
(612) 666-7204

PROFESSIONAL **EXPERIENCE:**	REAL ESTATE FINANCE PRACTICE. Real estate financing transactions, including construction financing, refinancings, municipal finance, revolving facilities, securtizing real estate collateral in multistate asset based transactions, leveraged buyouts, loan restructuring, loan workouts, deeds in lieu of foreclosure, nonjudicial foreclosures. Other experience includes negotiating legal aspects of purchase and sale of an equestrian center and lease negotiations. General real estate and corporate work.

EMPLOYMENT:

February 1992 to Present	**Oppenheimer, Wolff & Donnelly** Minneapolis, Minnesota Associate.
November 1989 to January 1992; Summer 1988	**Dorsey & Whitney** Minneapolis, Minnesota Associate.

EDUCATION:	**University of Minnesota Law School** Minneapolis, Minnesota J.D. 1989 Class Rank: Top 8%
	Ohio State University Columbus, Ohio B.A. *cum laude,* English, 1986 G.P.A.: 3.8/4.0

BAR ADMISSION:	State Bar of Minnesota, 1989.

PERSONAL INTERESTS:	Basketball, softball, golf, world travel, real estate investment, and stock speculation.

REFERENCES AVAILABLE UPON REQUEST

NANCY HUGHES-NELSON
129 Ocean View Road
Sausalito, California 94965
(415) 332-9436

EMPLOYMENT:

April 1991 to Present	**Grubb & Ellis Company**

San Francisco, California
<u>Attorney</u>. Real estate financing transactions, including construction financing, refinancings, securitizing real estate collateral in asset-based transactions, leveraged buyouts, loan restructuring, loan workouts, judicial and nonjudicial foreclosures.

November 1987
to March 1991;
Summer 1986

Pillsbury, Madison & Sutro
San Francisco, California
<u>Real Estate Finance Associate.</u>

EDUCATION:

University of California, at Berkeley
Boalt Hall
Berkeley, California
J.D. 1987
<u>Class Rank:</u> Top 15%
Member, <u>California Law Review</u>

Harvard University
Cambridge, Massachusetts
B.A. *summa cum laude*, Political Science, 1984
<u>G.P.A.:</u> 4.0/4.0

BAR ADMISSION: State Bar of California, 1987.

PERSONAL INTERESTS: Wine tasting and tennis.

REFERENCES AVAILABLE UPON REQUEST

GLORIA BERMAN
3785 West Beach Road
Miami, Florida 33131
(305)   577-7821

EDUCATION:

Cornell University Law School
Ithaca, New York
J.D. 1990
Class Rank: Top 12%
Note & Comment Editor, Cornell Law Review

Smith College
Northampton, Massachusetts
B.A. *magna cum laude*, Political Science, 1987.
G.P.A.: 3.85/4.0

EMPLOYMENT:

March 1992 to Present;
November 1990 to
February 1992;
Summer 1989

Weil, Gotshal & Manges
Miami, Florida;
New York, New York
Real Estate Litigation Associate. Involved in law and motions
practice, discovery, settlement negotiations, and research in
matters including appointment and termination of receivers,
breaches of commercial leases, and breach of contract.

BAR ADMISSIONS: State Bars of New York, 1990; Florida 1992.

PERSONAL INTERESTS: Sailing and tennis.

REFERENCES AVAILABLE UPON REQUEST

ALEXANDER THURN
416 D Street
San Diego, California 92101
(619) 724-8213

EMPLOYMENT:

October 1991 to Present	**Gray, Cary, Ames & Frye** San Diego, California Real Estate Litigation Associate. Involved in law and motions practice, discovery, settlement negotiations, and research in matters including appointment and termination of receivers, breaches of commercial leases, and breach of contract. Represent estate in an Action to Set Aside a Deed.
Summer 1990	**Honorable Terry McWalters** Superior Court of San Diego Extern.
Summer 1989	**District Attorney's Office** San Diego, California Extern.

EDUCATION:

University of San Diego School of Law
San Diego, California
J.D. 1991
Class Rank: Top 5%
Note & Comment Editor, San Diego Law Review.

University of Arizona
Tucson, Arizona
B.S. *cum laude*, Accounting, 1988.
G.P.A.: 3.6/4.0

BAR ADMISSION: State Bar of California, 1991.

PERSONAL INTERESTS: Bowling and golf.

REFERENCES AVAILABLE UPON REQUEST

STEPHANIE FEIN
34 Village Drive
New York, New York 10022
(212)   845-2414

EMPLOYMENT:

October 1993
to Present

Shearman & Sterling
New York, New York
Securities & Antitrust Litigation Associate. Involved in several
$100 million securities litigation cases. Extensive deposition and
discovery experience. Draft pretrial briefs and motions.
Perform pretrial preparation. Second chaired several trials.
Negotiate settlements.

October 1991
to September 1993;
Summer 1989

White & Case
New York, New York
Commercial Litigation Associate.

EDUCATION:

University of Chicago Law School
Chicago, Illinois
J.D. 1991
Class Rank: Top 15%
Note & Comment Editor, University of Chicago Law Review

State University of New York, at Buffalo
Buffalo, New York
B.A. *summa cum laude*, Political Science, 1988

BAR ADMISSION: State Bar of New York, 1991.

PERSONAL INTERESTS: Running marathons, aerobics, and tennis.

REFERENCES AVAILABLE UPON REQUEST

ROBERT H. SWANN
590 Lake Forest Drive
Chicago, Illinois 60602
(312)   977-5694

PROFESSIONAL **EXPERIENCE:**	<u>SECURITIES & ANTITRUST LITIGATION PRACTICE.</u> Involved in complex securities litigation cases. Take and defend depositions. Involved in all phases of discovery. Draft pretrial briefs and motions. Perform pretrial preparation. Extensive trial experience. Negotiate and draft settlement agreements.

EDUCATION:

University of Pennsylvania Law School
Philadelphia, Pennsylvania
J.D. 1988
<u>Class Rank:</u> Top 11%
Member, <u>University of Pennsylvania Law Review</u>

Princeton University
Princeton, New Jersey
B.A. *summa cum laude*, Philosophy, 1985

EMPLOYMENT:

June 1993 to Present	**Jenner & Block** Chicago, Illinois <u>Associate.</u>
October 1991 to May 1993	**Mayer, Brown & Platt** Chicago, Illinois <u>Associate.</u>
October 1988 to September 1991; Summer 1987	**Schnader, Harrison, Segal & Lewis** Philadelphia, Pennsylvania <u>Associate.</u>

BAR ADMISSIONS: State Bars of Pennsylvania, 1988; Illinois 1991.

PERSONAL INTERESTS: Jogging and ice hockey.

REFERENCES AVAILABLE UPON REQUEST

SALLY BROWN
8712 Forsyth Boulevard, Apt. 705
St. Louis, Missouri 63105
(314) 314-2777

EMPLOYMENT:

January 1993 to Present	**May Department Stores Company** St. Louis, Missouri <u>Director of Labor Relations</u>. Responsible for entire corporation labor activities including negotiations of all labor agreements, labor litigation and arbitration, day-to-day grievance handling and contract administration, organizational campaigns and supervisory training on all aspects of labor/employee relations, multiemployer pension plan withdrawal liability issues, acquisitions, and divestitures.
March 1987 to December 1992	**Armstrong, Teasdale, Schlafly & Davis** St. Louis, Missouri <u>Partner 1990-1992; Associate 1987-1990.</u>
October 1983 to February 1987	**National Labor Relations Board** St. Louis, Missouri (Region 14) <u>Field Attorney/Trial Specialist.</u> Responsibilities included all aspects of litigation in unfair labor practice cases and federal court injunction hearings. Trial preparation included writing complaints and other formal documents, pleadings, and witness preparation. Additional responsibilities included investigation and analysis of unfair labor practice charges and representation petitions, conducting hearing and elections, and drafting Decisions and Directions of Elections.

EDUCATION:

St. Louis University School of Law
St. Louis, Missouri
J.D. *cum laude*, 1983
Member, <u>Public Law Review</u>

George Washington University
Washington, DC
B.A. *magna cum laude*, Sociology, 1980
<u>G.P.A.:</u> 3.7/4.0

BAR ADMISSION: State Bar of Missouri, 1983.

PERSONAL INTERESTS: Gourmet cooking and gardening.

REFERENCES AVAILABLE UPON REQUEST

FRANCIS HOUSTON
4910 Massachusetts Avenue
Washington, DC 20036
(202)   758-7066

PROFESSIONAL EXPERIENCE:	<u>LABOR PRACTICE.</u> Experience includes both traditional labor and employment law. Draft opinion letters on various aspects of labor law including ERISA, ADEA, OWBPA, COBRA, wage and hour law, and drug testing; EEOC and DFEH position statements; legal memoranda on various labor issues including arbitrations. Litigation experience includes drafting motions for summary judgment, interrogatories, subpoenas, demands for documents, briefs, and various other motions and pleadings.

EMPLOYMENT:

September 1990 to Present	**Arent, Fox, Kintner, Plotkin & Kahn** Washington, DC <u>Associate.</u>
August 1988 to August 1990; Summer 1987	**Covington & Burling** Washington, DC <u>Associate.</u> Offer Extended.
EDUCATION:	**College of William & Mary, School of Law** Williamsburg, Virginia J.D. 1988 <u>Class Rank:</u> #1 in the class Editor in Chief, <u>William & Mary Law Review</u> <u>Honors:</u> American Jurisprudence Awards in Evidence, Real Property, Civil Procedure, Torts, and Criminal Procedure. **University of Maryland** College Park, Maryland B.A. Political Science, 1985 <u>G.P.A.:</u> 3.7/4.0 <u>Honors:</u> Outstanding Student Award; Dean's Honor List 1983-1985.
BAR ADMISSIONS:	State Bars of Virginia and District of Columbia, 1988.
PERSONAL INTERESTS:	Ceramic sculpting.

REFERENCES AVAILABLE UPON REQUEST

PAUL McMULLEN
1612 Laurel Canyon Boulevard
North Hollywood, California   91604
(818)   680-2213

**PROFESSIONAL
EXPERIENCE:**

<u>LABOR EMPLOYMENT PRACTICE.</u> Draft and review personnel policies, employment law training, day-to-day legal advice and assistance, labor arbitrations, EEO discrimination charges, wage and hour compliance, wrongful discharge defense, and employee benefit claims. Supervise outside counsel and staff of five legal professionals.

EMPLOYMENT:

February 1987 to
Present

Nestle U.S.A., Inc.
Glendale, California
<u>Senior Counsel.</u>

August 1985 to
January 1987

Littler, Mendelson, Fastiff & Tichy
Los Angeles, California
<u>Associate.</u>

October 1976 to
July 1985

Star-Kist Food, Inc.
Long Beach, California
<u>Corporate and Labor Counsel.</u>

EDUCATION:

University of Southern California Law Center
Los Angeles, California
J.D. 1976
<u>Class Standing:</u> Top 20%

University of California, Los Angeles
Los Angeles, California
B.S. *cum laude*, Mathematics, 1973
<u>G.P.A.:</u> 3.8/4.0

BAR ADMISSION: State Bar of California, 1976.

PERSONAL INTERESTS: Karate.

REFERENCES AVAILABLE UPON REQUEST

CAROLYN RIGOLETTO
4770 Main Street
Austin, Texas 73343
(512) 897-6545

EDUCATION:	**University of Texas at Austin School of Law** Austin, Texas J.D. 1987 - With Honors Rank: Top 13% **Boston University** Boston, Massachusetts B.S. *cum laude*, Broadcasting and Film, 1984

EMPLOYMENT:

September 1987 to Present	**Blazier, Rutland & Lerner** Austin, Texas Labor & Employment Associate. Extensive experience in all aspects of management labor relations, including federal and state court trial and appellate practice in employment discrimination actions; wrongful terminations; wage and hour disputes; arbitrations; trade secret litigation; drafting personal service agreements, personnel handbooks, and policies. Draft opinion letters on various aspects of ERISA, ADEA, OWBPA, COBRA, and drug testing; EEOC and DFEH position statements.
Summer 1986	**Long, Burner, Parks & Sealy** Austin, Texas Summer Associate. Offer extended.
Summer 1985	**Scanlan & Buckle** Austin, Texas Summer Associate.

BAR ADMISSION:	State Bar of Texas, 1987.
PERSONAL INTERESTS:	Photography and tennis.

REFERENCES AVAILABLE UPON REQUEST

PARTNER-LEVEL RESUMES

While many partner level attorneys feel that their achievement and status speak for itself, a potential employer still prefers a formal resume. As before, a one-page resume is preferable. However, partners, due to their years of experience, often need to have a two-page resume. The Professional Experience paragraph needs to be as explicit as possible. However, unlike the associate resume, the partner seeking new employment usually has an additional opportunity to provide supplemental documents that will support why he or she should be hired. Such documents may include a client list (actual client names), the previous year's billings, projected billings for the current year, as well as new client prospects. These new sources of information are usually provided after the first resume has been submitted, and an initial meeting has taken place, where there was mutual interest.

We feel that the following partner-level resumes will assist you in preparing your resume.

CARLOS CRUZ
1901 Fifteenth Street NW
Washington, DC   20036
(202)   870-0303

PROFESSIONAL **EXPERIENCE:**	<u>**BUSINESS LITIGATION PRACTICE.**</u> Principally involved in defense of securities fraud claims, bank fraud, corporate and partnership dissolution, representation of automobile dealers and trade secret misappropriation issues. Represent computer industry companies in defense of breach of warranty claims and antitrust issues. Responsibilities include supervision matters in office and firm management activities.

EMPLOYMENT:

June 1982 to Present	**Crowell & Moring** Washington, DC <u>Partner 1986 to Present: Associate 1982-1986</u>
November 1978 to May 1982; Summer 1977	**Coudert Brothers** Washington, DC <u>Associate.</u>

EDUCATION:	**Cornell University Law School** Ithaca, New York J.D. 1978 <u>Class Rank:</u> Top 11% Member, <u>Cornell International Law Journal</u>
	Hofstra University Hempstead, New York B.A. *magna cum laude*, Latin Studies, 1975 <u>G.P.A.:</u> 3.7/4.0

PROFESSIONAL
AFFILIATIONS:

1986 to Present	Member, American Society of International Law
1984 to Present	Member, American Law Institute
1980 to Present	Member, Council on Foreign Relations
1983 to 1984	Member, American Bar Association, Section of Litigation, Committee on Litigation Management and Economics

1976 to 1977   Member, Association of Business Trial Lawyers
                        Member, Board of Governors; Program Chair

BAR ADMISSIONS: State Bars of New York; District of Columbia, 1978.

LANGUAGE: Fluent in Spanish.

PERSONAL INTERESTS: Latin art, literature, and history.

REFERENCES AVAILABLE UPON REQUEST

RALPH J. MARCONI, JR.
17643 University Street
Philadelphia, Pennsylvania   19103
(215)   968-2555

PROFESSIONAL EXPERIENCE:	<u>**BUSINESS LITIGATION PRACTICE.**</u> Representation of secured lenders, banks, and other commercial clients (individual and institutional) in state and federal cases. Broad experience in contract, tort and employment litigation; prejudgment remedies; appeals; representation of secured and unsecured creditors in bankruptcy courts; arbitration; corporate and partnership dissolutions.

EMPLOYMENT:

January 1987 to Present	**Morgan, Lewis & Bockius** Philadelphia, Pennsylvania <u>Partner 1989 to Present; Associate 1987-1989</u>
November 1984 to December 1986	**Pepper, Hamilton & Scheetz** Philadelphia, Pennsylvania <u>Associate.</u>
1983 to 1984	**Honorable Gerald M. Peabody** U.S. District Court for the Eastern District of Pennsylvania <u>Law Clerk</u>.

EDUCATION:	**University of Pennsylvania Law School** Philadelphia, Pennsylvania J.D. 1983 <u>Class Rank;</u> Top 15% Note & Comment Editor, <u>University of Pennsylvania Law Review</u>
	New York University New York, New York B.A. *summa cum laude*, Political Science, 1980 <u>G.P.A.;</u> 3.9/4.0

PROFESSIONAL AFFILIATIONS:

1993 to Present	Chairman, Philadelphia Bar Association
1992	Volunteer for the Indigent Program
1991	Civil Rights Committee

BAR ADMISSION: State Bar of Pennsylvania, 1983.

PERSONAL INTERESTS: Basketball, baseball, and football.

REFERENCES AVAILABLE UPON REQUEST

MARTIN A. WATANABE
2919 West Monroe Street
Chicago, Illinois 60603
(312) 336-1340

PROFESSIONAL **EXPERIENCE:**	**CORPORATE/BANKING PRACTICE.** Extensive experience includes mergers and acquisitions and banking transactions and federal securities regulation. Merger and acquisition practice involves wide variety of stock and asset acquisitions, mergers of both public and private companies, primarily for Japanese and British clients. Represent bank and financial institutions, both domestic and foreign, in credit enhancement transactions and in asset securitizations and leveraged buyout loans. Securities practice includes public offerings (representing both issuers and underwriters), private placements, corporate restructurings, venture capital financings, and foreign company offerings. Bank financings include letter of credit backstops for public financings. Involved with tender offers, and investment company matters.

EMPLOYMENT:

November 1982 to Present; Summer 1981	**Mayer, Brown & Platt** Chicago, Illinois Partner 1990 to Present; Associate 1982-1990.

EDUCATION:	**Northwestern University School of Law** Chicago, Illinois J.D. 1982 Order of the Coif Editor, Northwestern University Law Review **University of Chicago** Chicago, Illinois B.A. *summa cum laude*, English, 1979 G.P.A.: 3.8/4.0

BAR ADMISSION:	State Bar of Illinois, 1982.

PERSONAL INTERESTS:	Racquetball and squash.

REFERENCES AVAILABLE UPON REQUEST

DANIEL HARVEY
217 California Avenue
Palo Alto, California 94306
(415) 475-8729

PROFESSIONAL **EXPERIENCE:**	<u>**CORPORATE INTERNATIONAL PRACTICE.**</u> Representation of national and international companies that are leaders in commerce and industry. Specialization in cross-border corporate partnering, merger-acquisition and emerging company business transactions. Act as bioscience counsel for technology sectors: biotechnology, biomedical, medical devices, diagnostics, healthcare services, pharaceutical, and agritechnology.

EMPLOYMENT:

April 1986 to Present	**Wilson, Sonsini, Goodrich & Rosati** Palo Alto, California <u>Partner.</u>
June 1980 to March 1986	**Graham & James** San Francisco, California <u>Partner 1982-1986; Associate 1980-1982.</u>
November 1975 to May 1980	**Baker & McKenzie** Chicago, Illinois <u>Associate.</u>

EDUCATION:	**University of Chicago** Chicago, Illinois J.D. 1975 <u>Class Rank:</u> Top 8% Editor, <u>University of Chicago Law Review</u>
	Indiana University/Bloomington School of Law Bloomington, Indiana B.S. *summa cum laude*, Biology, 1972 <u>G.P.A.:</u> 3.9/4.0

BAR ADMISSIONS:	State Bars of Illinois, 1975; California, 1980.

PERSONAL INTERESTS:	Jogging and tennis.

REFERENCES AVAILABLE UPON REQUEST

RACHEL BROWN-GILBERT
824 Ninth Street
Santa Monica, California 90402
(310) 895-7832

EMPLOYMENT:

July 1988 to Present	**Brown & Wood** Los Angeles, California Partner 1991 to Present; Associate 1988-1991. Represent companies in corporate transactions including debt restructuring, "going private" transactions, issuer tender offers, acquisitions, "back door" public offerings, bank or investor financings and distribution arrangements. Recent transactions have included a $40 million corporate reorganization structured as an acquisition of assets from related partnerships; related "going private" filings with the Securities and Exchange Commission; an exchange offer involving publicly issued debentures and hybrid securities; a $5 million issuer tender offer for Units in exchange for Common Stock; acting as U.S. counsel in a public offering in Canada; and credit facilities ranging from $2,500,000 to $20 million. Also advise companies on general corporate matters such as distribution agreements, manufacturing financing, transfers of restricted stock and listing on an exchange and on securities-regulation matters such as short-swing profits rules and SEC filings.
March 1984 to June 1988	**Whitaker Corporation** Los Angeles, California Corporate Counsel. Experience included mergers and acquisitions, public offerings, private placements, exchange offers, tender offers (hostile and friendly), leveraged buyouts, fairness opinions, joint venture arrangements, various types of financings (project financings, railroad equipment trust and conditional sales financings, and industrial revenue), corporate spin-offs, stock dividends, and stock splits, listings on stock exchanges, SEC proceedings and litigation, corporate trust indenture responsibility, and venture capital transactions.
November 1979 to February 1984	**Kinsella, Boesch, Fujikawa & Towle** Los Angeles, California Corporate Associate.

EDUCATION: **New York University School of Law**
                        New York, New York
                        J.D. 1979
                        Order of the Coif
                        Editor, New York University Law Review

                        Tufts University
                        Medford, Massachusetts
                        B.A. *summa cum laude*, History, 1976
                        G.P.A.: 3.9/4.0

BAR ADMISSION: State Bar of California, 1979.

PERSONAL INTERESTS: President, Board of Directors, Big Brothers/Big Sisters of
                        Los Angeles.

                        REFERENCES AVAILABLE UPON REQUEST

ANDREA RUBIN
16 Greenwich Avenue
New York, New York 10038
(212)   826-5121

PROFESSIONAL **EXPERIENCE:**	<u>CORPORATE SECURITIES PRACTICE.</u> Concentration in corporate and securities law with emphasis on corporate mergers, acquisitions, and other business combinations; corporate finance (particularly public and limited offerings of securities including debt and equity securities, including issuances of common stock, preferred stock and subordinated debentures) and general representation of public and privately held companies, including thrift institutions; special counsel to the issuer in the public offering of an aggregate of $2 billion of CMOs; representation of underwriters in private offerings of multifamily housing tax-free bonds; and representation of brokers and issuers in NASD and SEC investigations and administrative proceedings. Supervision of associates.

EMPLOYMENT:

1989 to Present   **Reboul, MacMurray, Hewitt, Maynard & Kristol**
New York, New York
<u>Partner.</u>

1982 to 1989   **Debevoise & Plimpton**
New York, New York
<u>Partner 1986-1989; Associate 1982-1986.</u>

1977 to 1982   **Skadden, Arps, Slate, Meagher & Flom**
New York, New York
<u>Associate.</u>

EDUCATION: **Harvard University Law School**
Cambridge, Massachusetts
J.D. 1977
<u>Class Rank:</u> Top 15%
Member, <u>Harvard Law Review</u>

Princeton University
Princeton, New Jersey
B.A. *summa cum laude*, Political Science, 1974
<u>G.P.A.:</u> 3.9/4.0

**PROFESSIONAL
ACTIVITIES:**

1978 to Present   Member, American Bar Association
                         Member, Corporate, Banking and Business Law Section

1978 to Present   Member, New York State Bar Association
                         Member, Business and Corporations Section

1978 to Present   Member, Women Lawyers' Association of New York
                         Member, Board of Governors 1980 to 1986
                         Treasurer, 1982 to 1984
                         Co-Chair, Appointive Office Committee 1981 to 1983

1978 to 1984   Member, Board of Governors
                         Harvard Law School Alumni Association

PUBLICATIONS:

1988   Author, "Takeovers--The Way of the Future," <u>Takeovers and
                         Mergers Business Journal</u> (1988).

1986   Author, "Securities Laws: Are They Too Lenient?" <u>Securities
                         Issues Journal</u> (1986).

BAR ADMISSION: State Bar of New York, 1977.

PERSONAL INTERESTS: Gourmet cooking and wine tasting.

REFERENCES AVAILABLE UPON REQUEST

PAUL WALKER
1431 McKinney Street
Houston, Texas 77010
(713)   623-0753

PROFESSIONAL
EXPERIENCE:

LABOR PRACTICE. Extensive experience in all aspects of management labor relations, including federal and state court trial and appellate practice in employment discrimination actions, wrongful terminations, wage and hour disputes, arbitrations, and trade secret litigation; drafting personal service agreements, personnel handbooks, and policies. Experience in IATSE negotiations, arbitration practice involving WGA and DGA disputes. Supervise all labor department associates and assign all litigation matters in firm's Houston office.

EMPLOYMENT:

December 1987
to Present

Fulbright & Jaworski
Houston, Texas
Partner.

October 1979
to November 1987

Strasburger & Price, L.L.P.
Dallas, Texas
Partner 1986-1987: Associate 1979-1986.

EDUCATION:

University of Texas, at Austin School of Law
Austin, Texas
J.D. 1979
Class Rank: Top 5%
Note & Comment Editor, Texas Law Review

Southern Methodist University
Dallas, Texas
B.A. *summa cum laude*, Economics, 1976
G.P.A.: 3.87/4.0

BAR ADMISSION
AND ACTIVITIES:

State Bar of Texas, 1979.
American Bar Association (Member, Sections on Labor and Employment Law; Litigation).

PERSONAL INTERESTS: Horseback riding.

REFERENCES AVAILABLE UPON REQUEST

Index